This book belongs to:

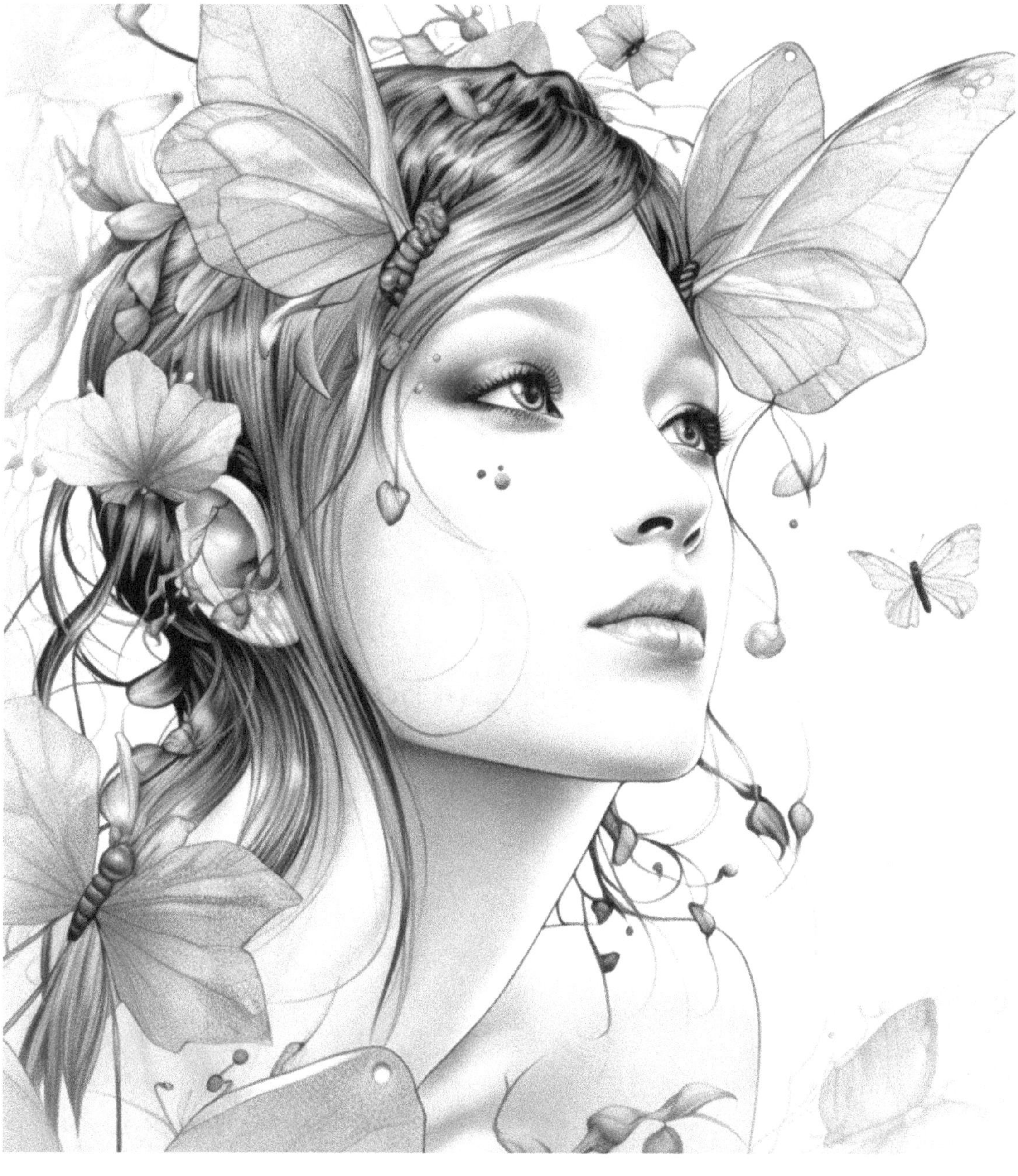

Thank you so much for choosing our coloring book!

We wanted to take a moment to express our gratitude for choosing the Forest Fairies coloring book.

It means so much to us that you have chosen to support our work, and we hope that this book brings you hours of joy and relaxation.

Creating these images was a labor of love for our team, and we are thrilled to know that they have found a home with you.

We truly believe that coloring is a wonderful way to unwind and de-stress, and we hope that you find that to be true as well.

Once again, thank you for your support. It is truly appreciated.

Enchanting Escapes Team

About Your new Book

Welcome to your new coloring book, "Forest Fairies"! This book is inspired by the enchanting world of fairies and their magical forests, featuring intricate illustrations that invite you to explore a world of fantasy and wonder.

We believe that coloring is not just for children, but can be a great way for adults to unwind and destress. Coloring in these beautiful fairy landscapes can help you relax and escape from the stresses of everyday life, allowing you to focus on the present moment and find inner peace.

We hope that this coloring book will inspire you to rediscover your creativity and imagination, while also providing a calming and meditative experience.

So grab your favorite coloring tools and let your inner artist take flight in the magical world of "Forest Fairies"!

If you enjoy this book, please let us and others know by leaving a review on Amazon :-)

Forest Fairies left this blank for you

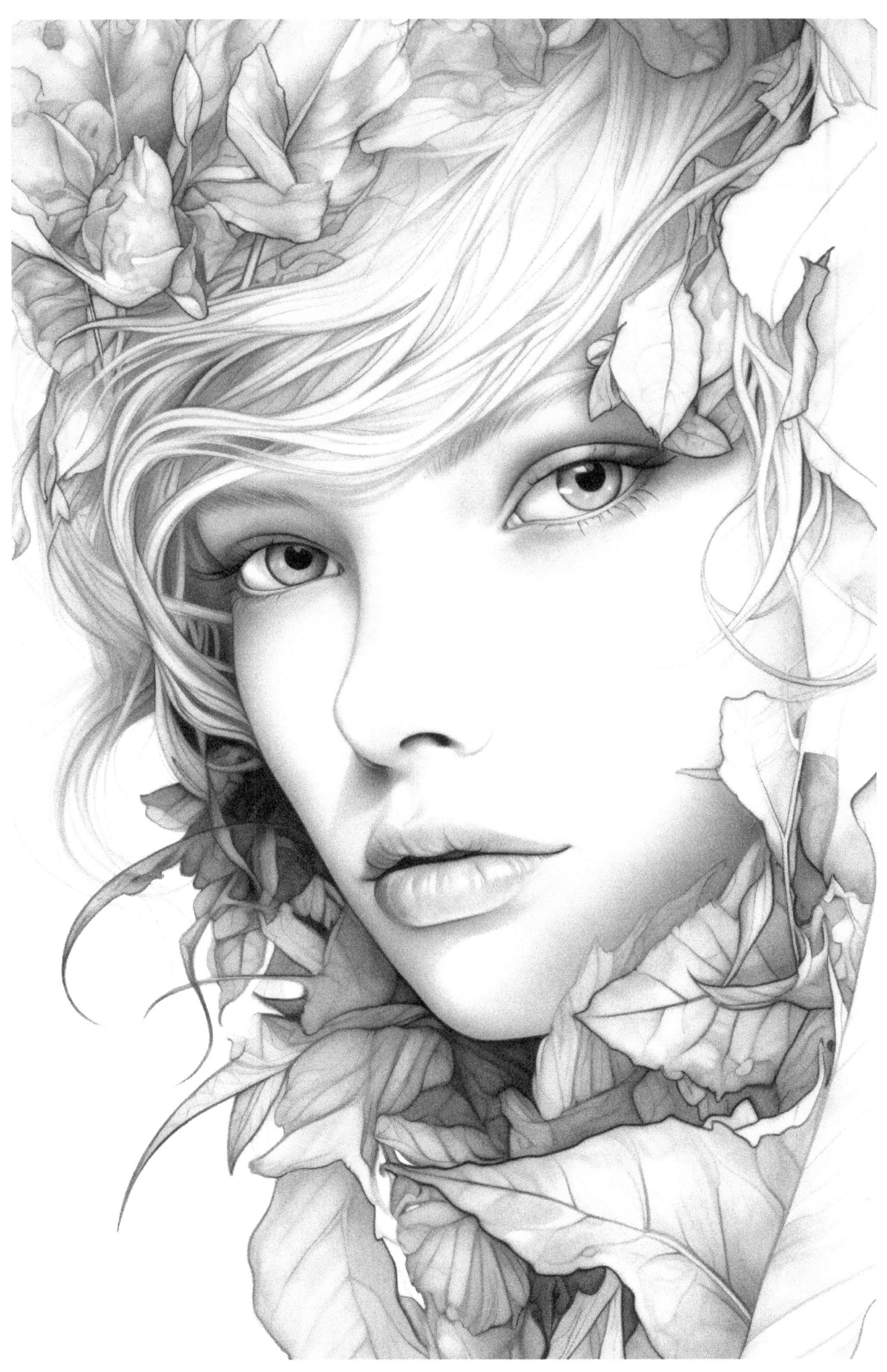

Forest Fairies left this blank for you

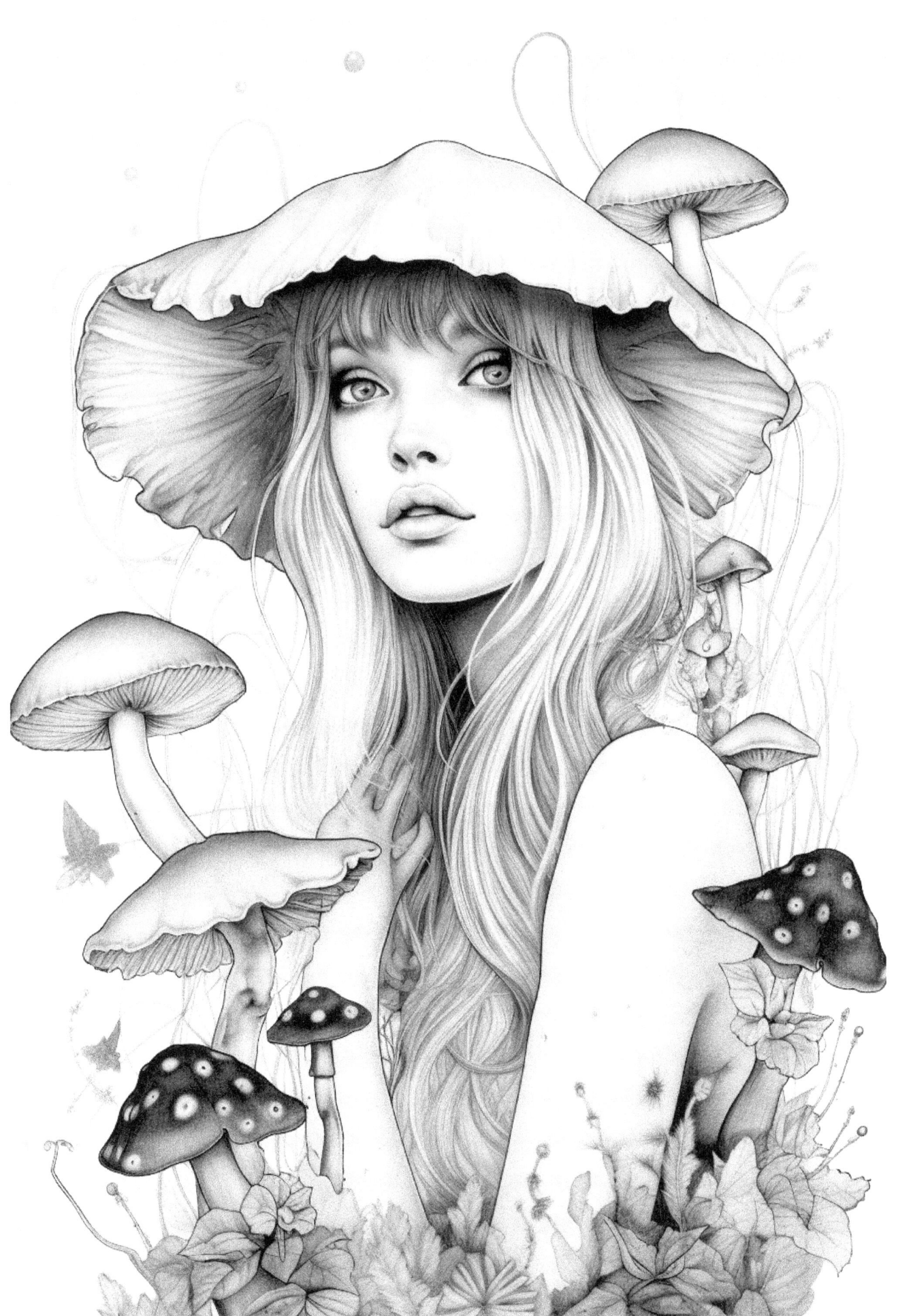

Forest Fairies left this blank for you

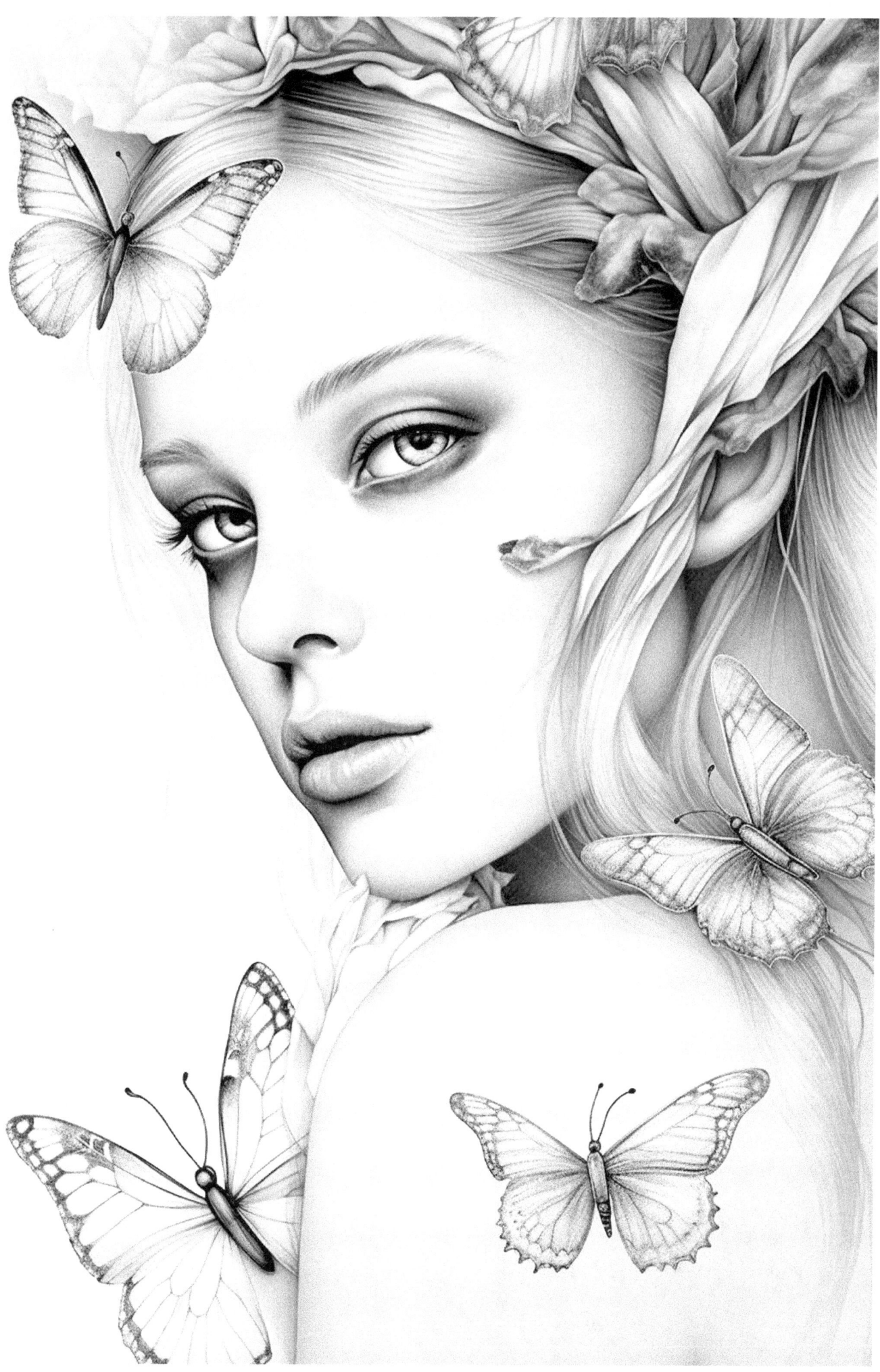

Forest Fairies left this blank for you

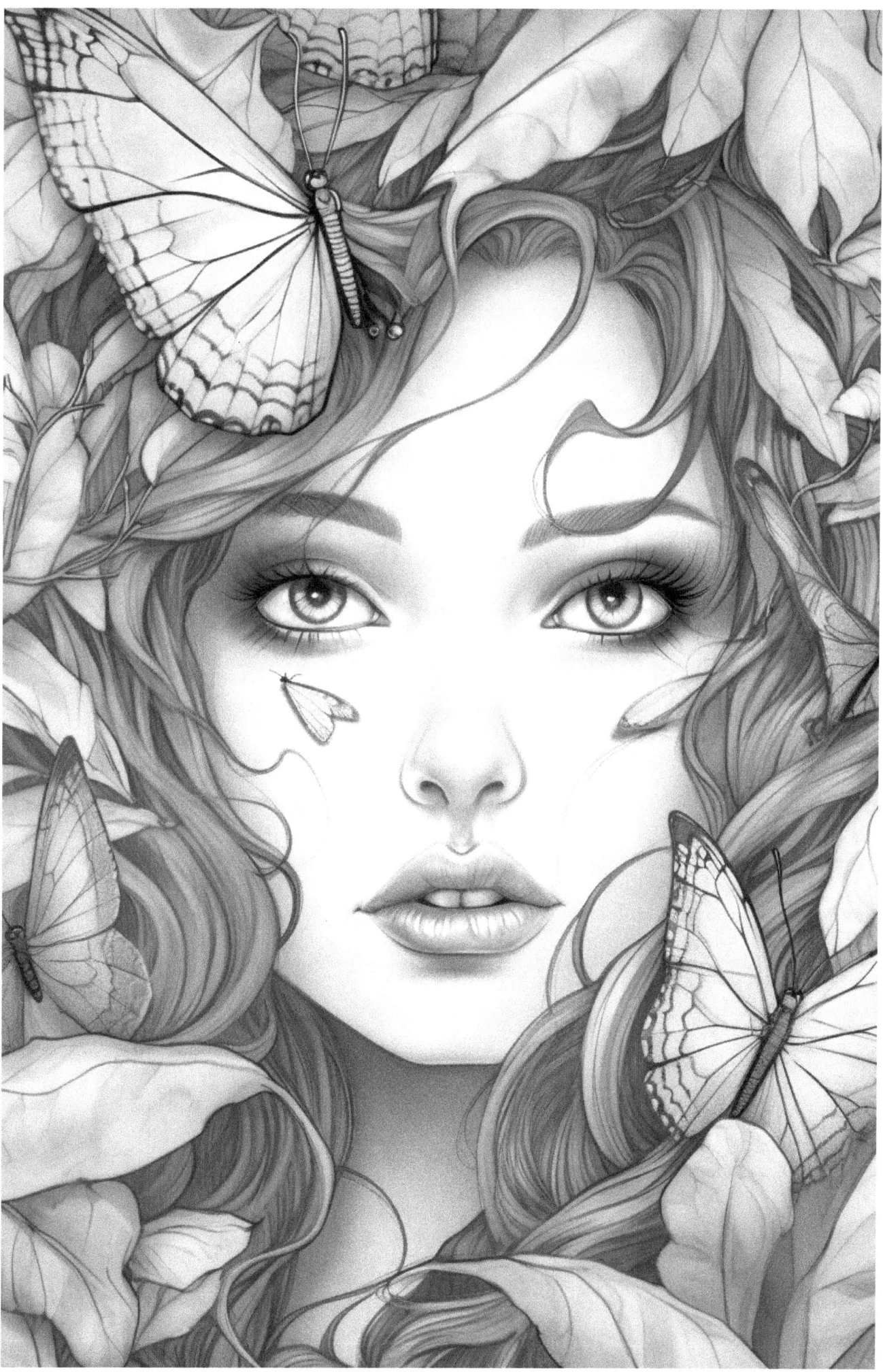

Forest Fairies left this blank for you

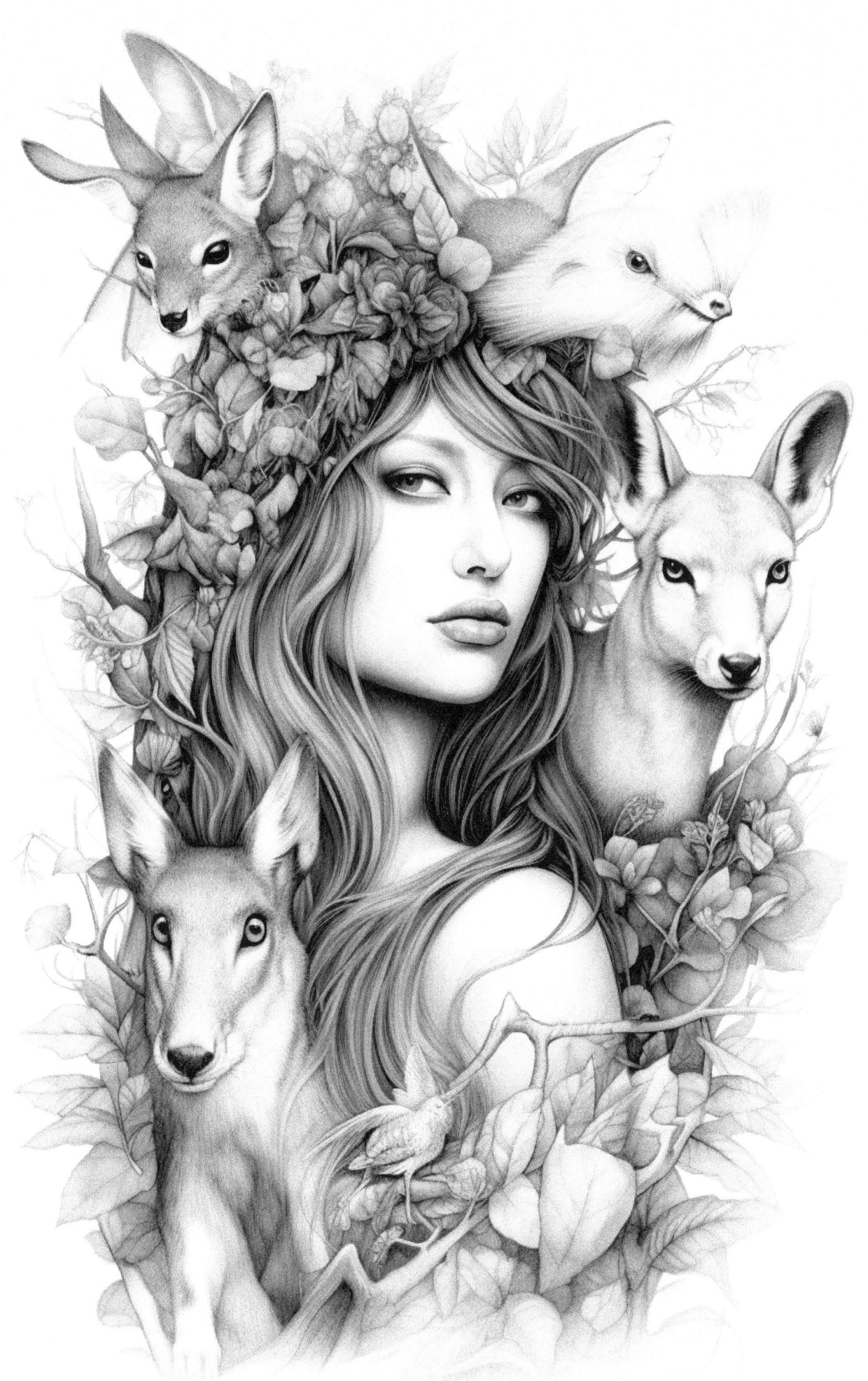

Forest Fairies left this blank for you

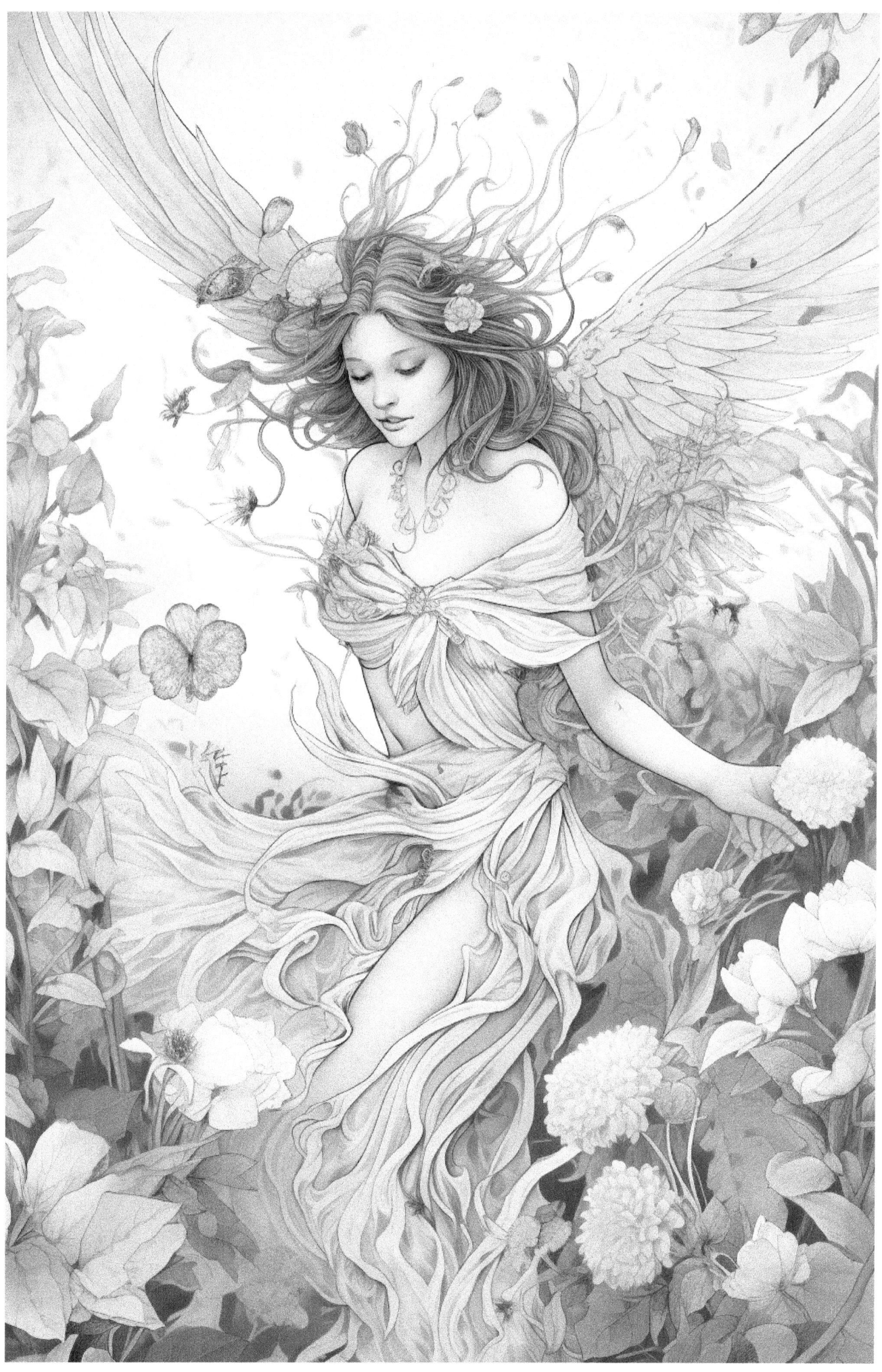

Forest Fairies left this blank for you

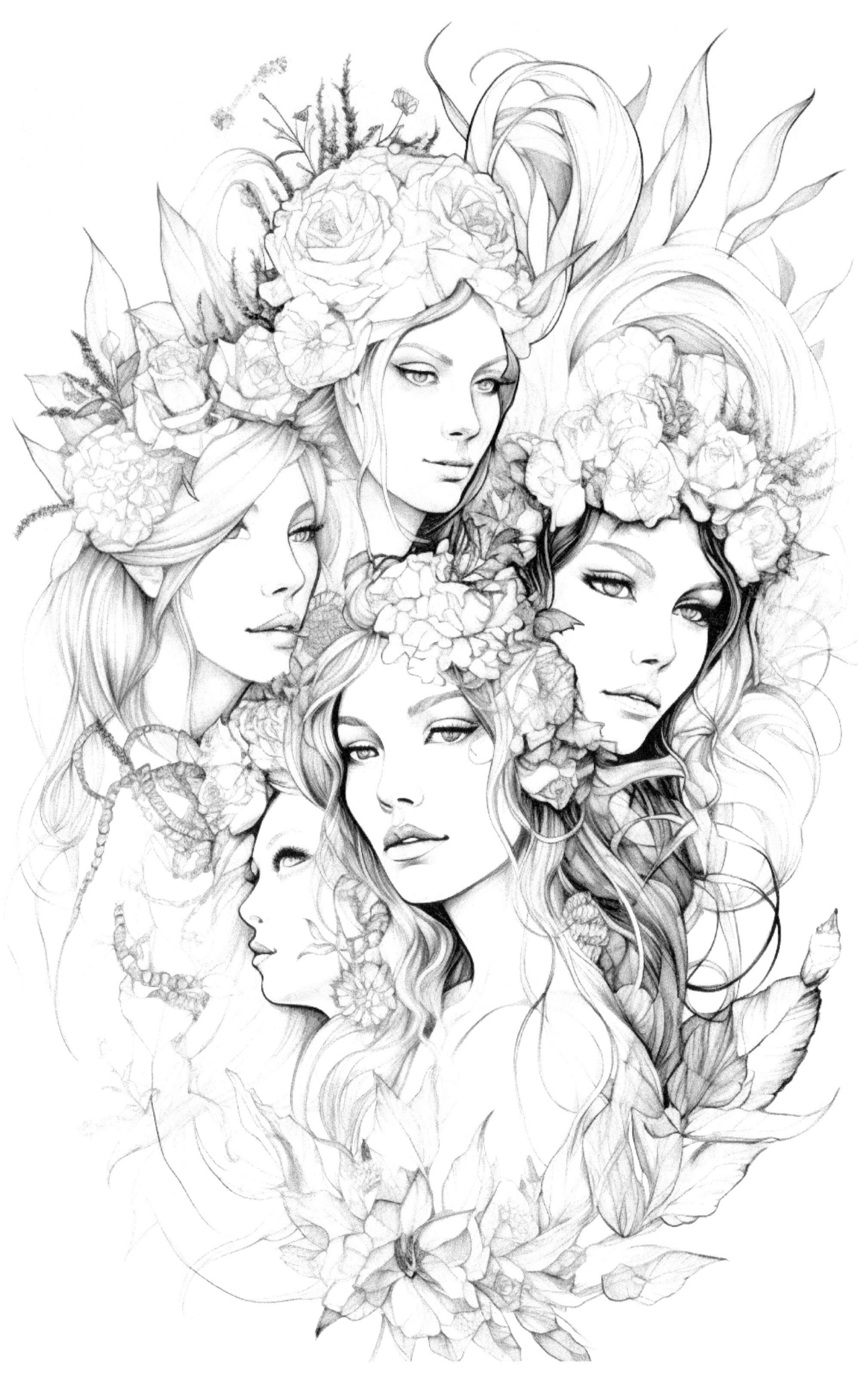

Forest Fairies left this blank for you

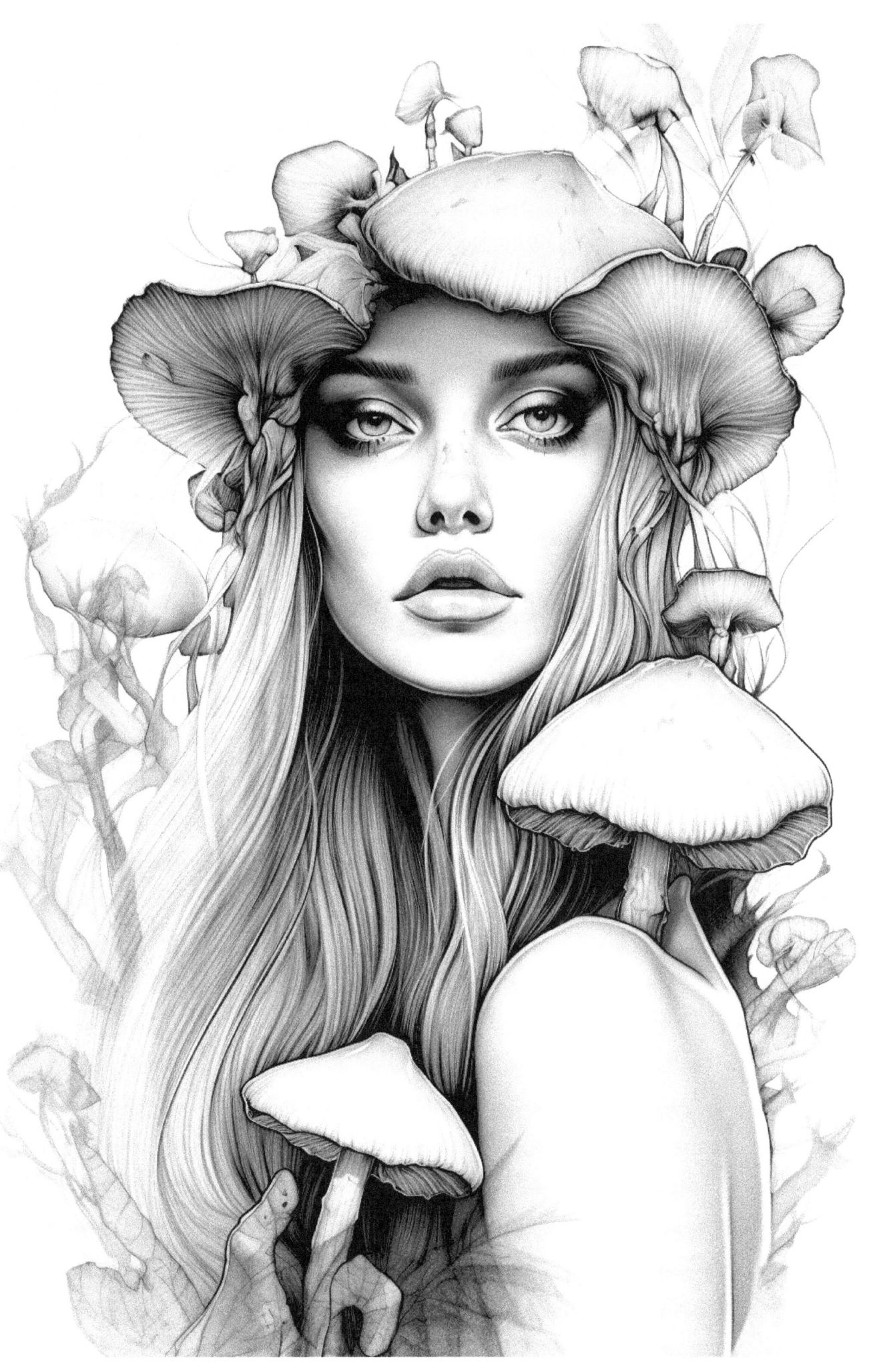

Forest Fairies left this blank for you

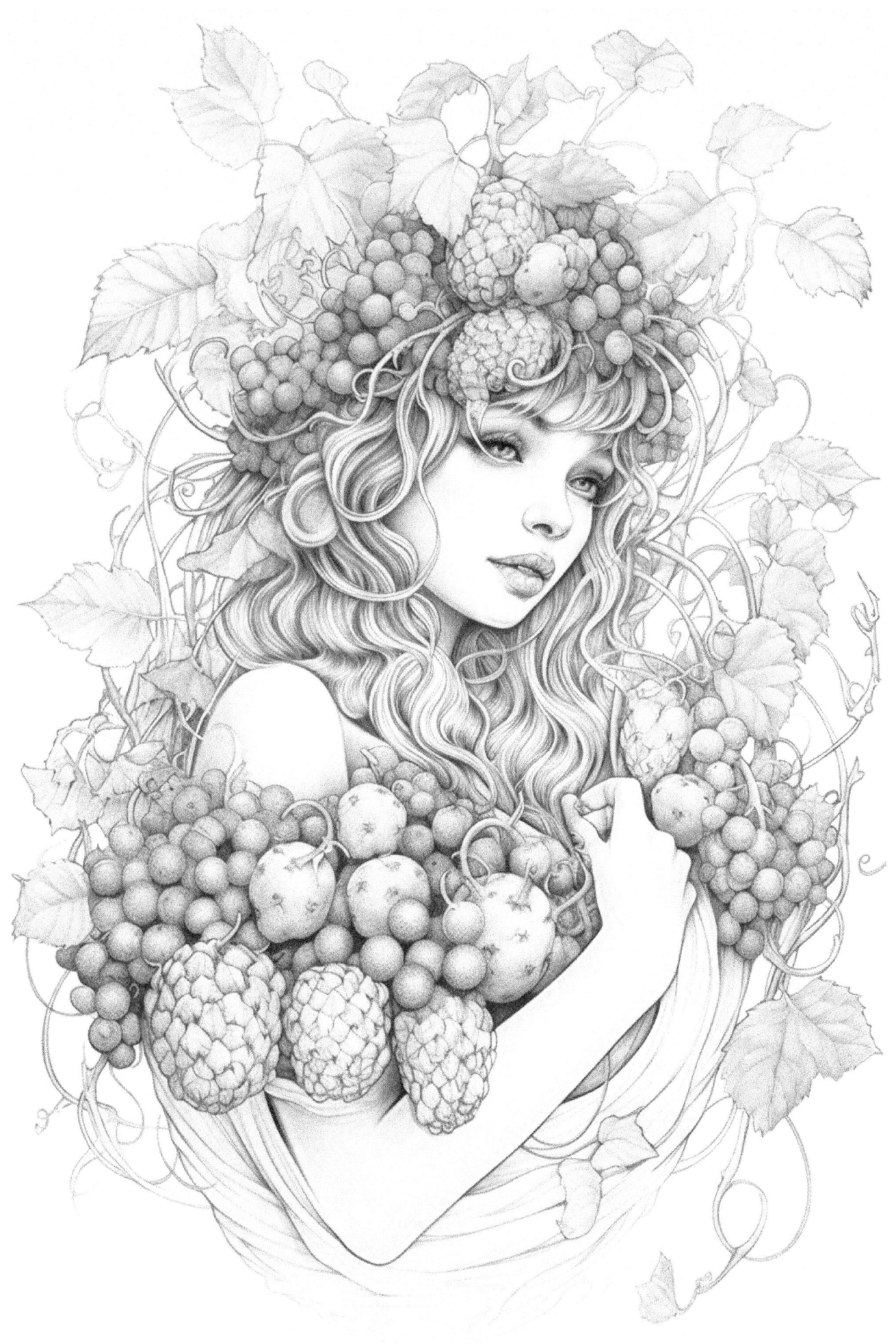

Forest Fairies left this blank for you

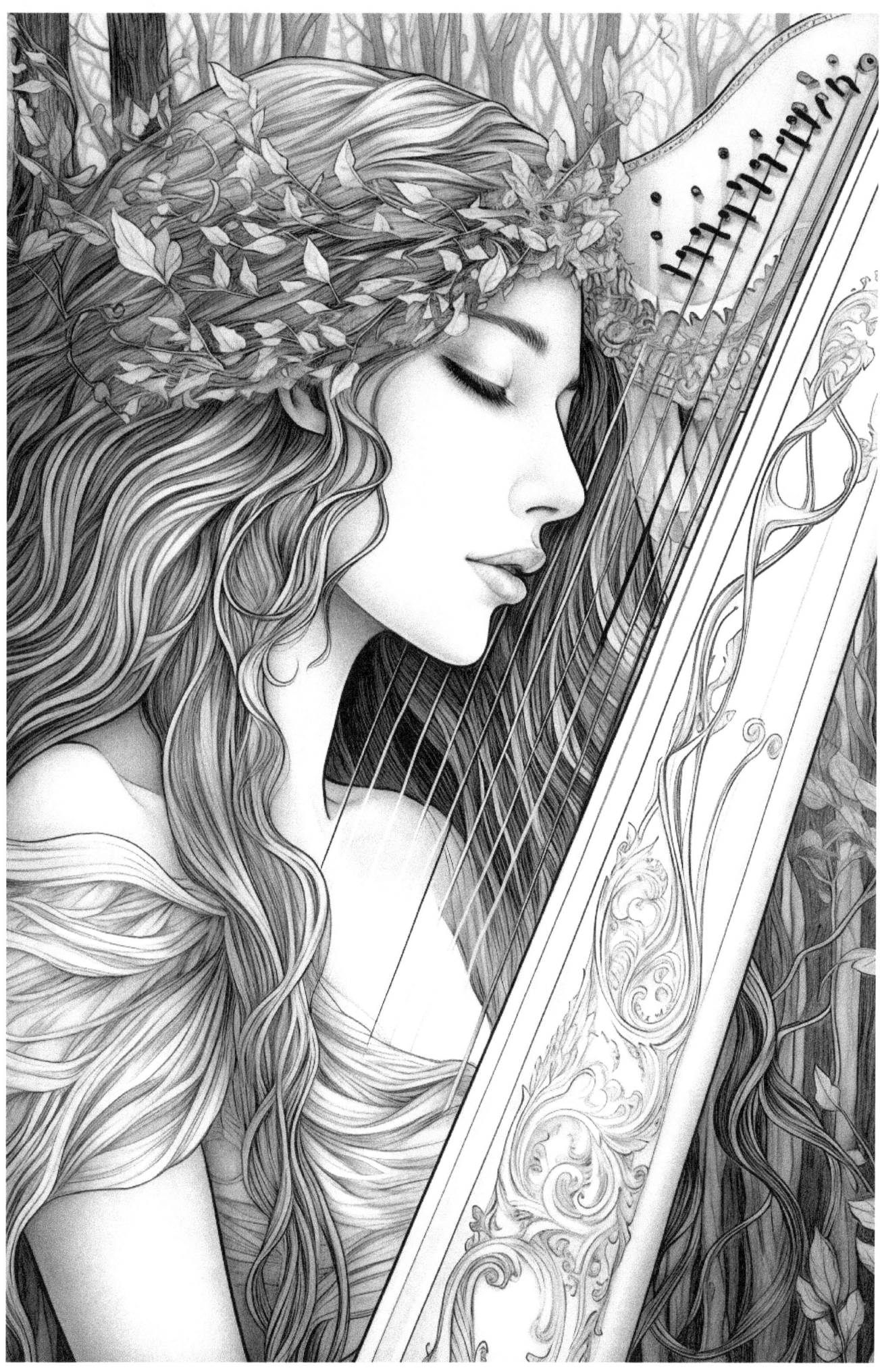

Forest Fairies left this blank for you

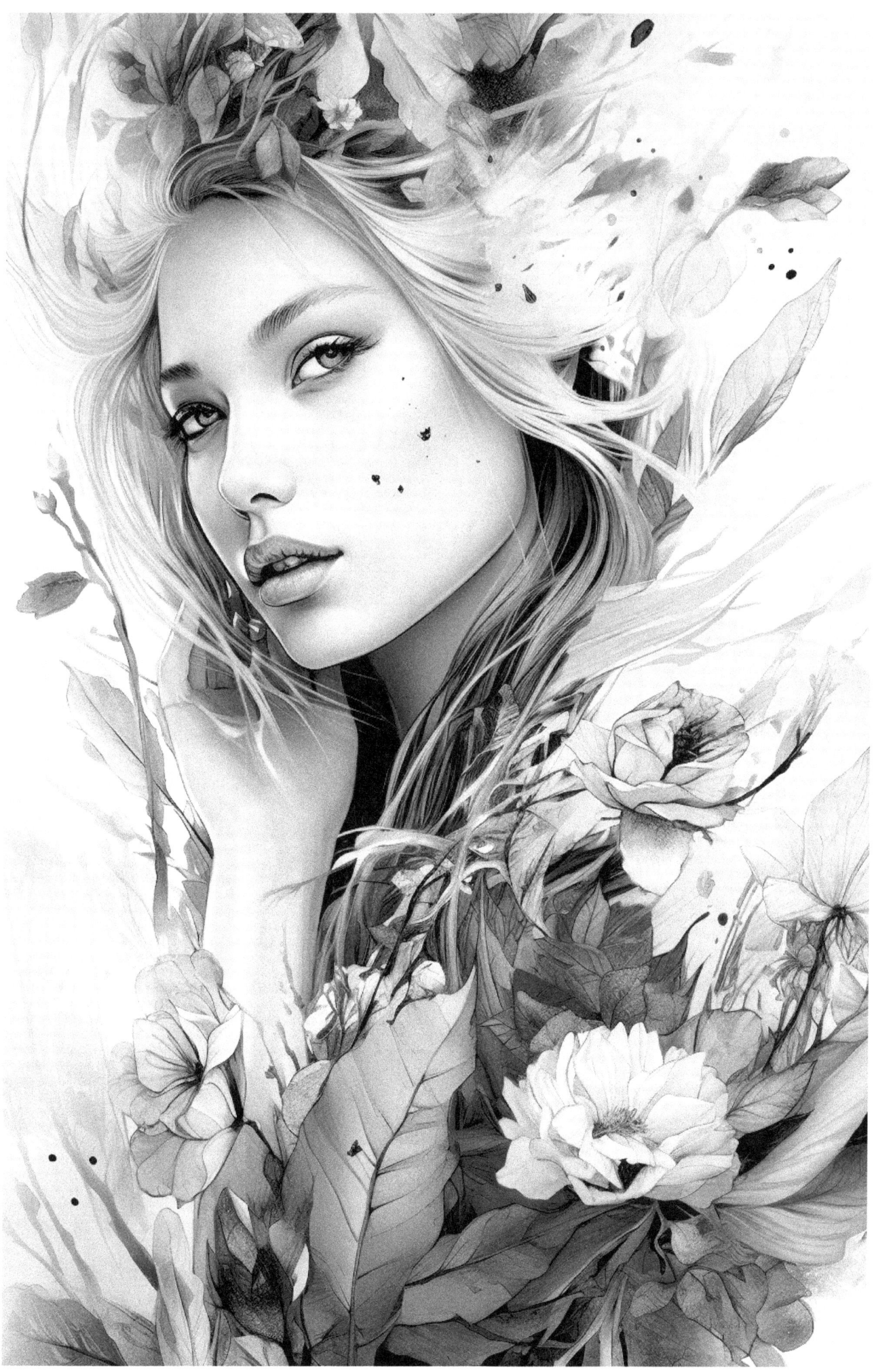

Forest Fairies left this blank for you

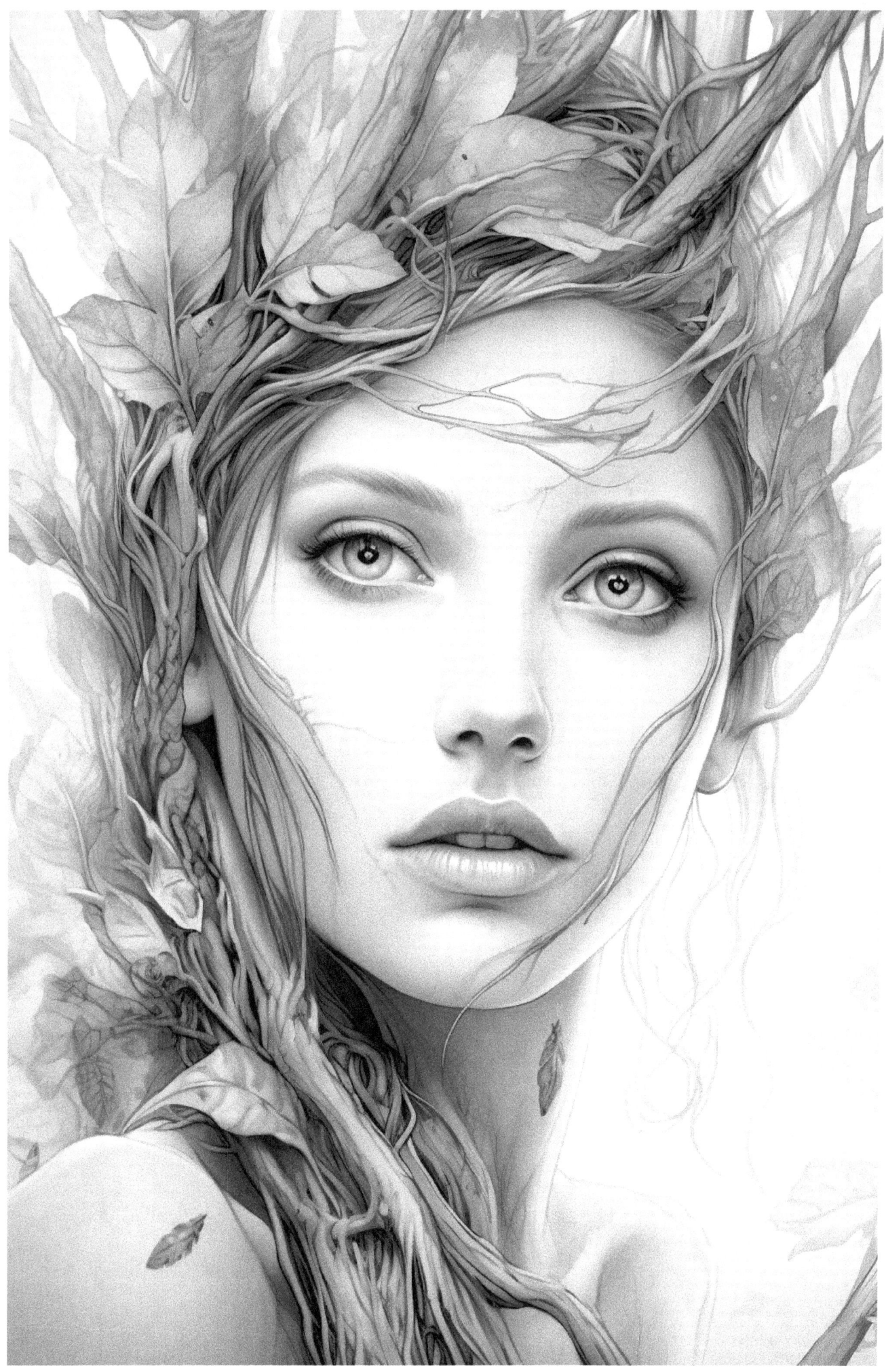

Forest Fairies left this blank for you

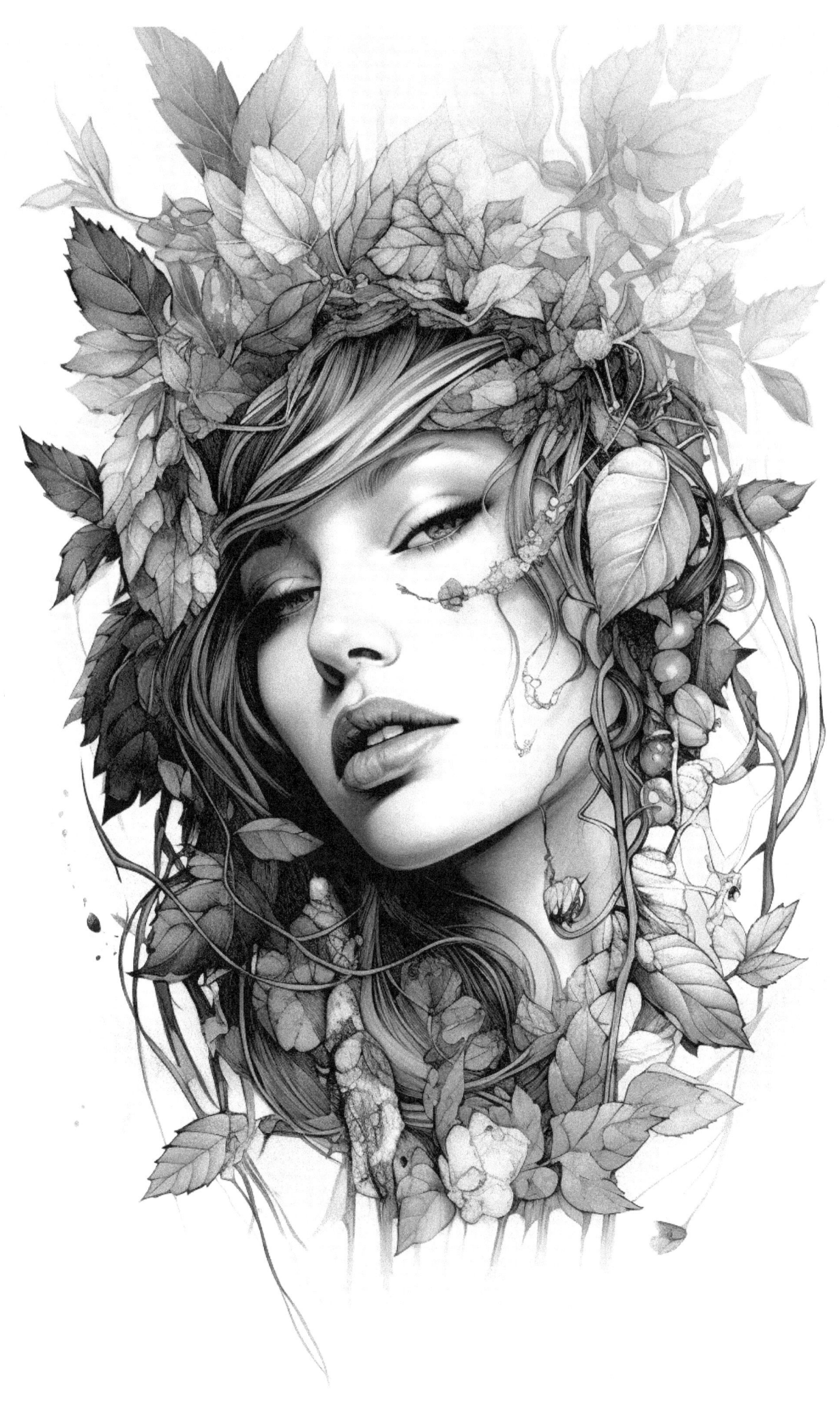

Forest Fairies left this blank for you

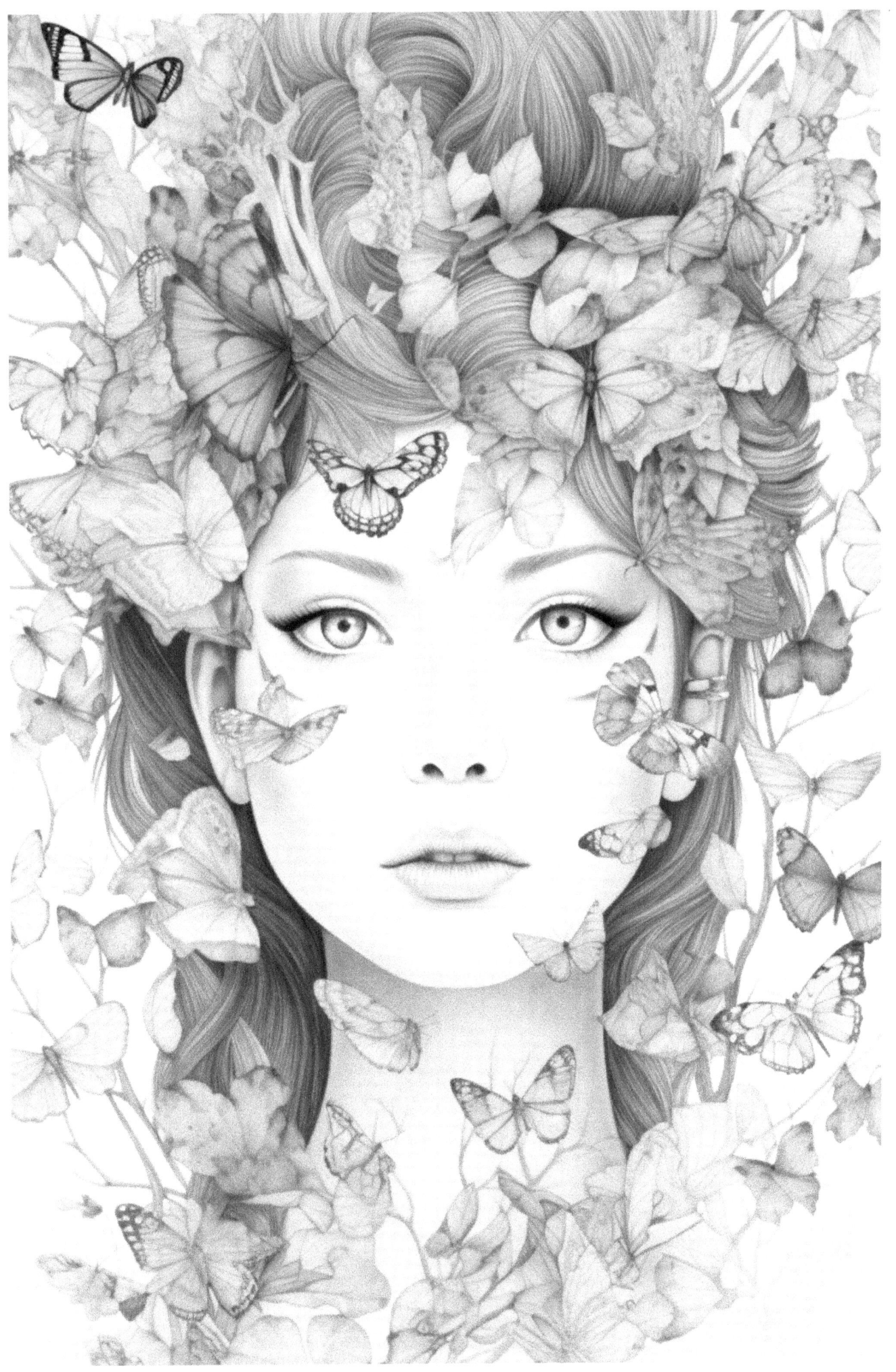

Forest Fairies left this blank for you

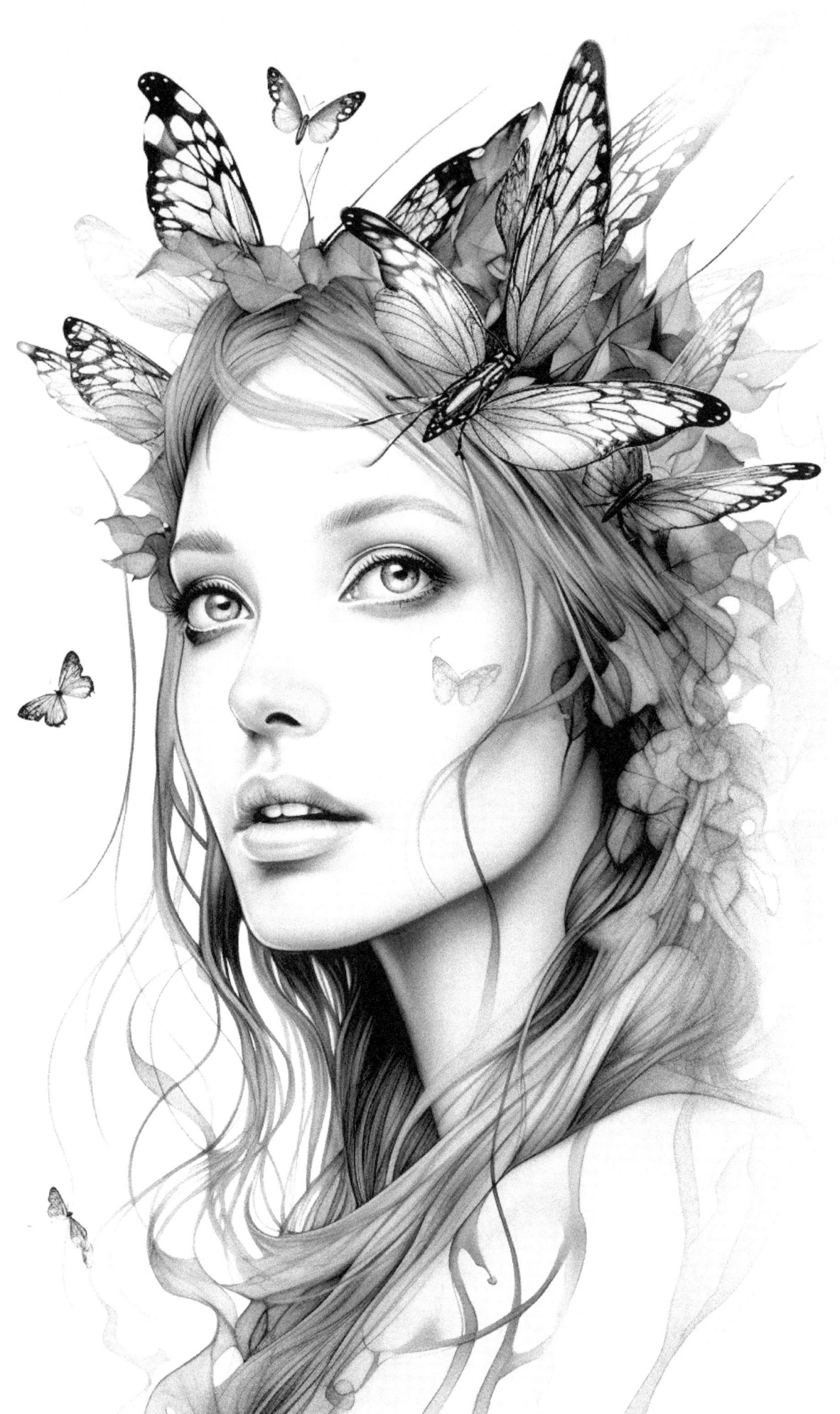

Forest Fairies left this blank for you

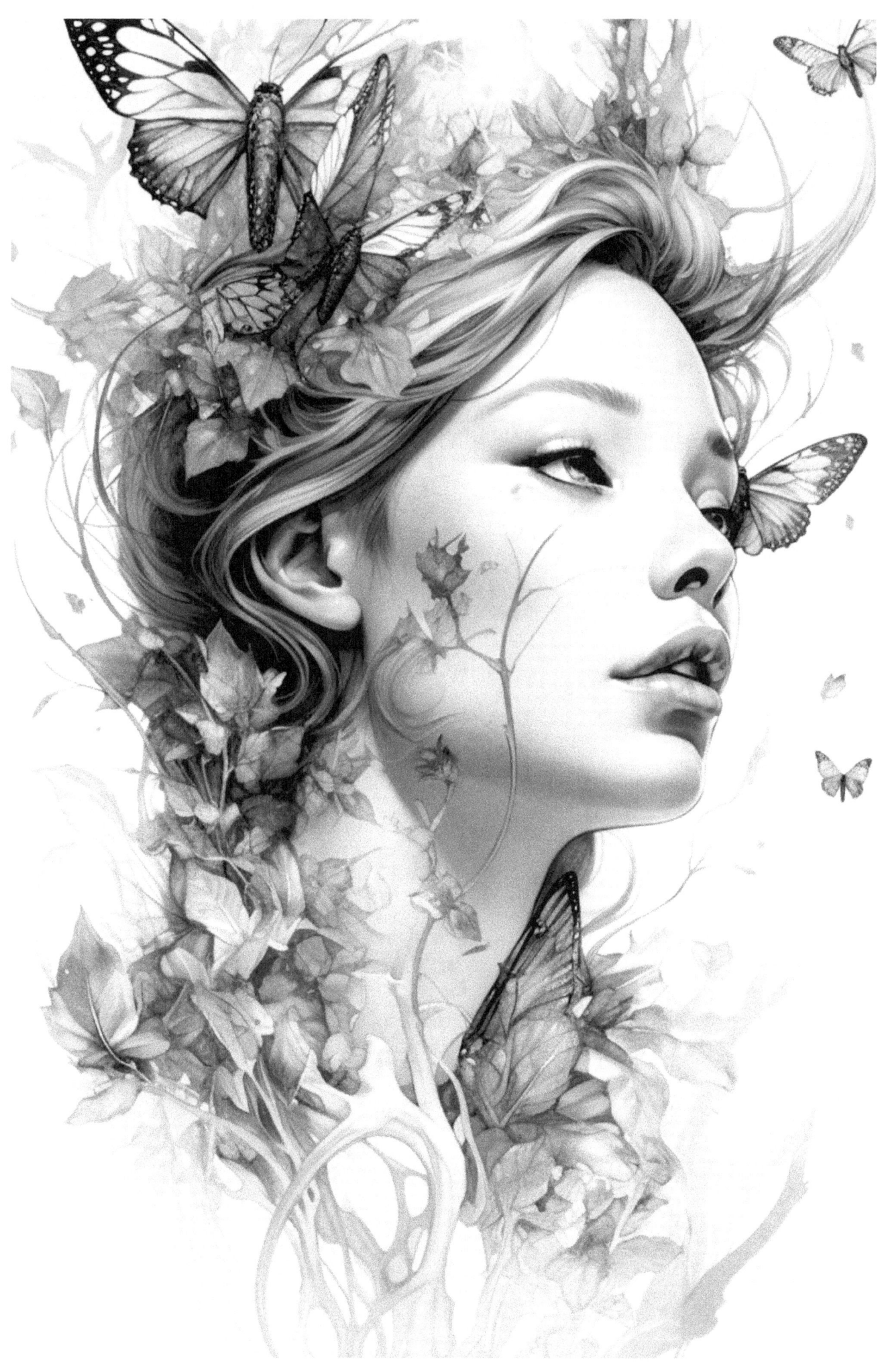

Forest Fairies left this blank for you

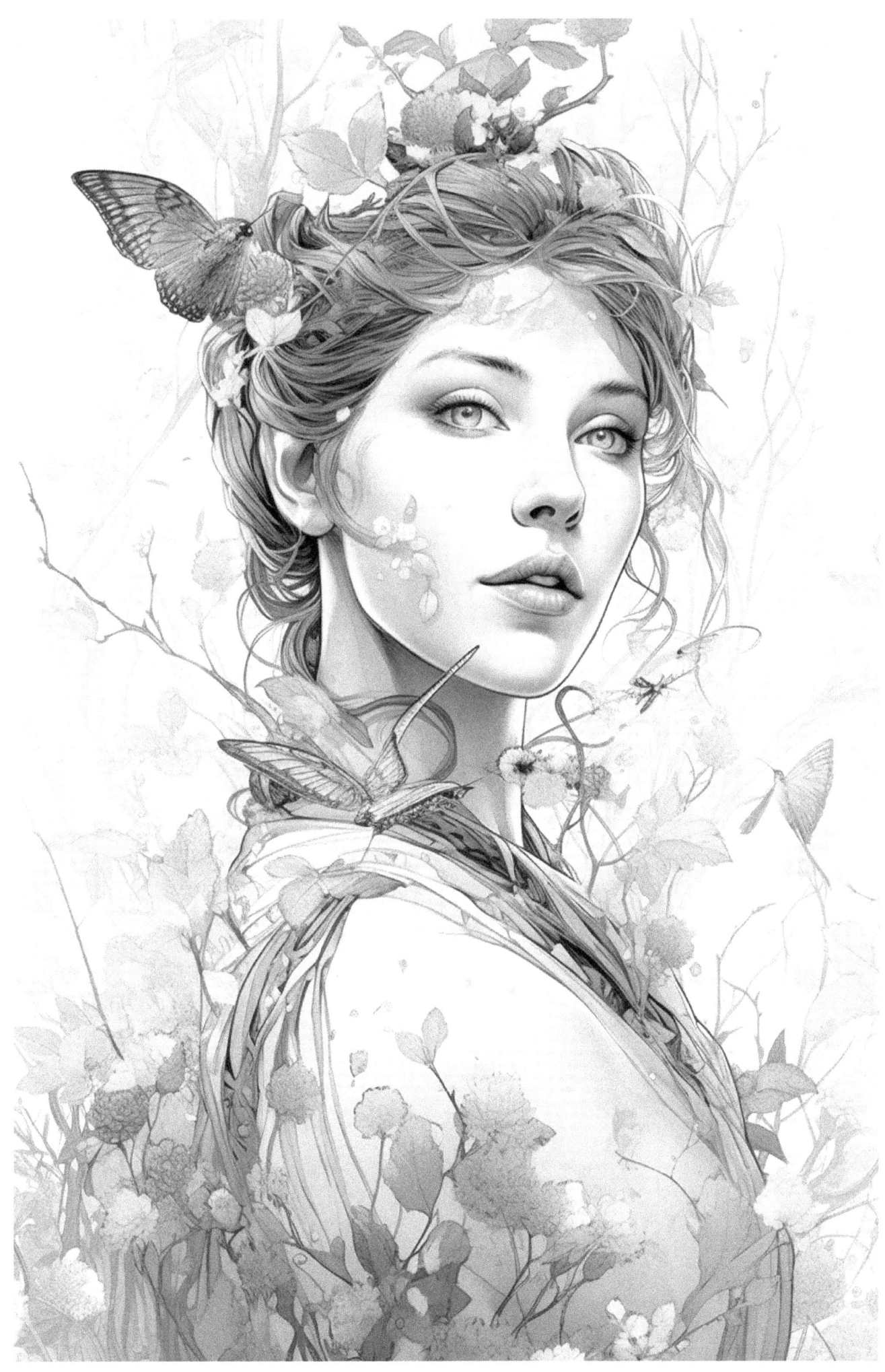

Forest Fairies left this blank for you

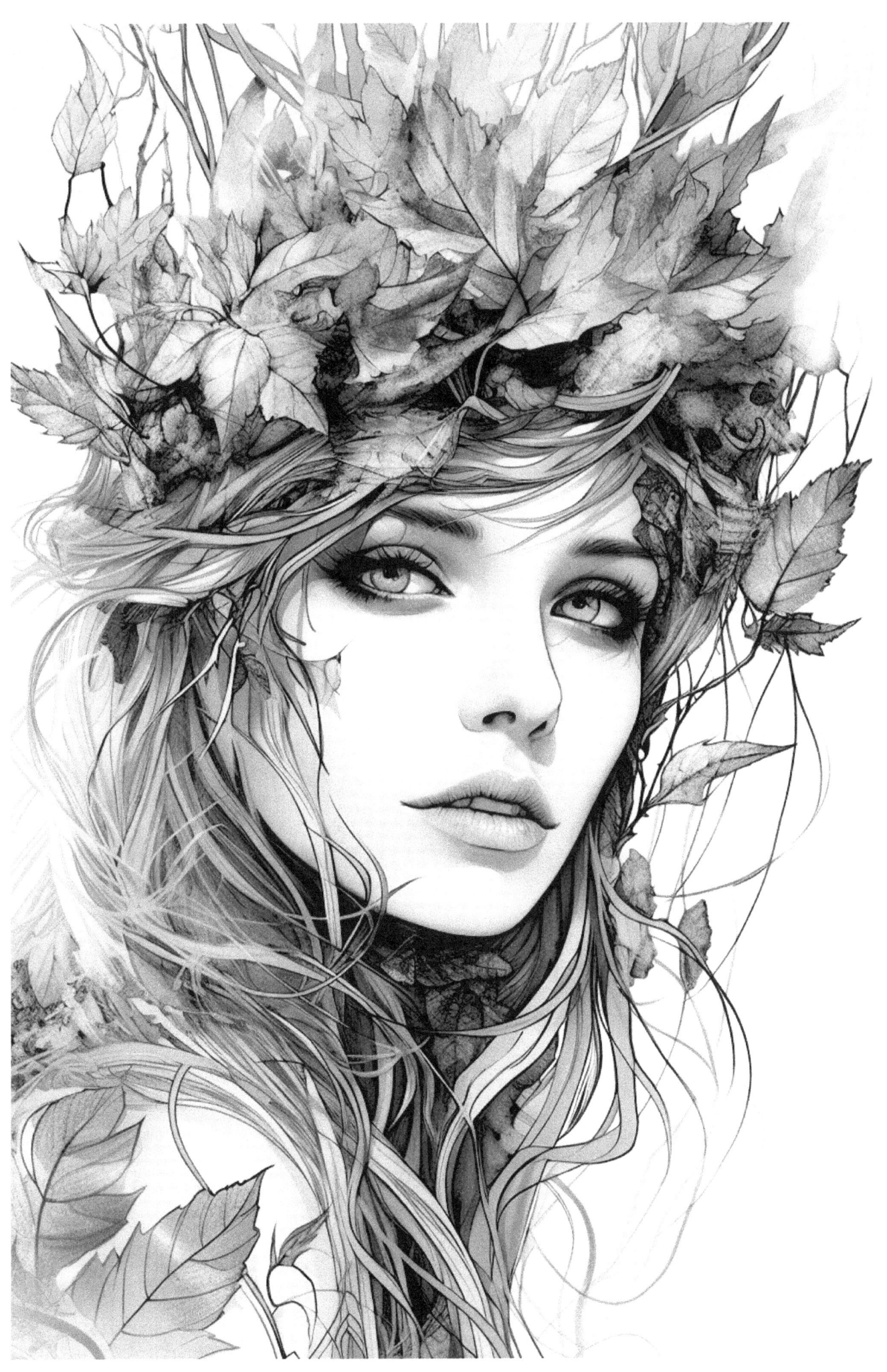

Forest Fairies left this blank for you

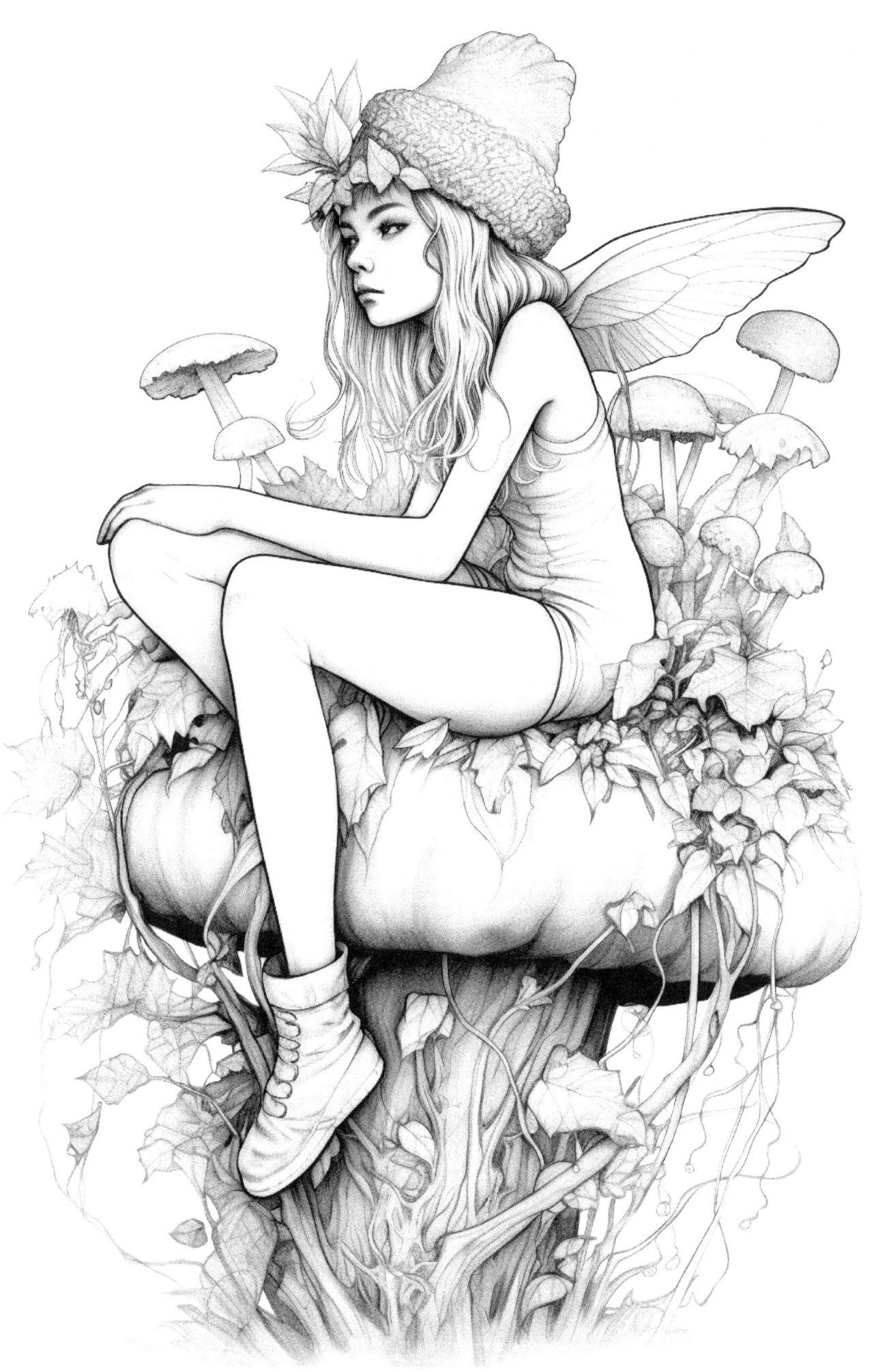

Forest Fairies left this blank for you

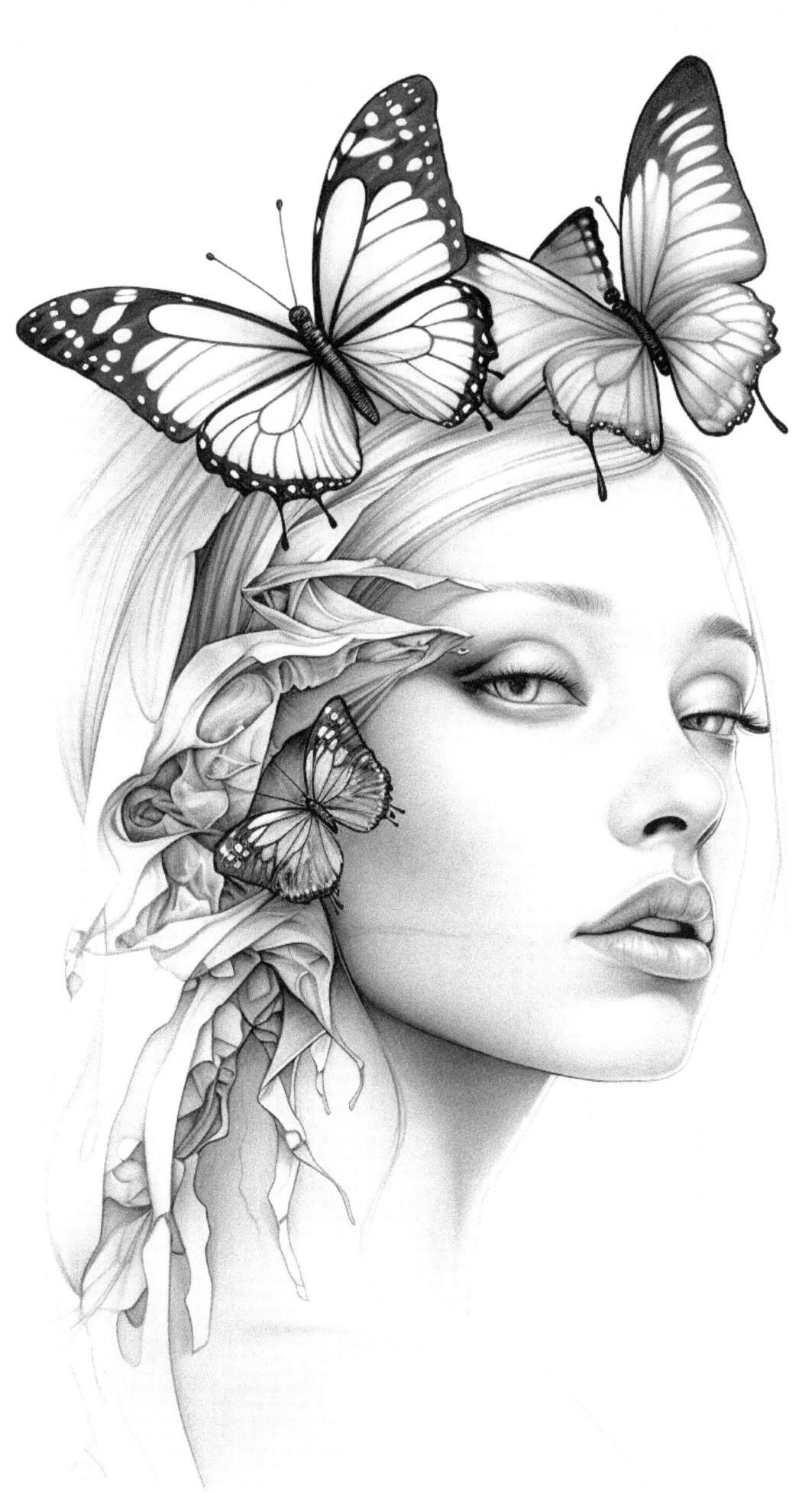

Forest Fairies left this blank for you

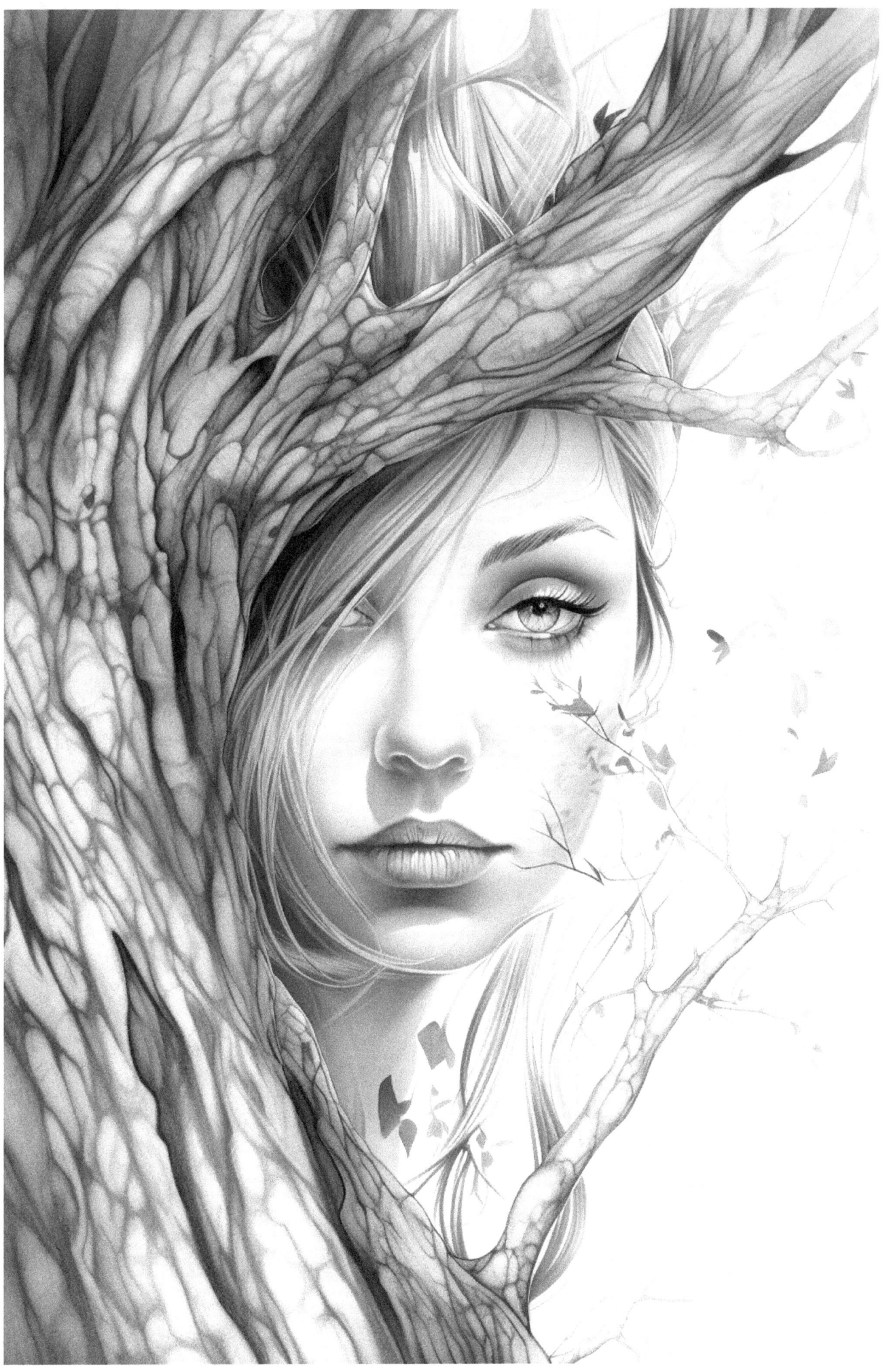

Forest Fairies left this blank for you

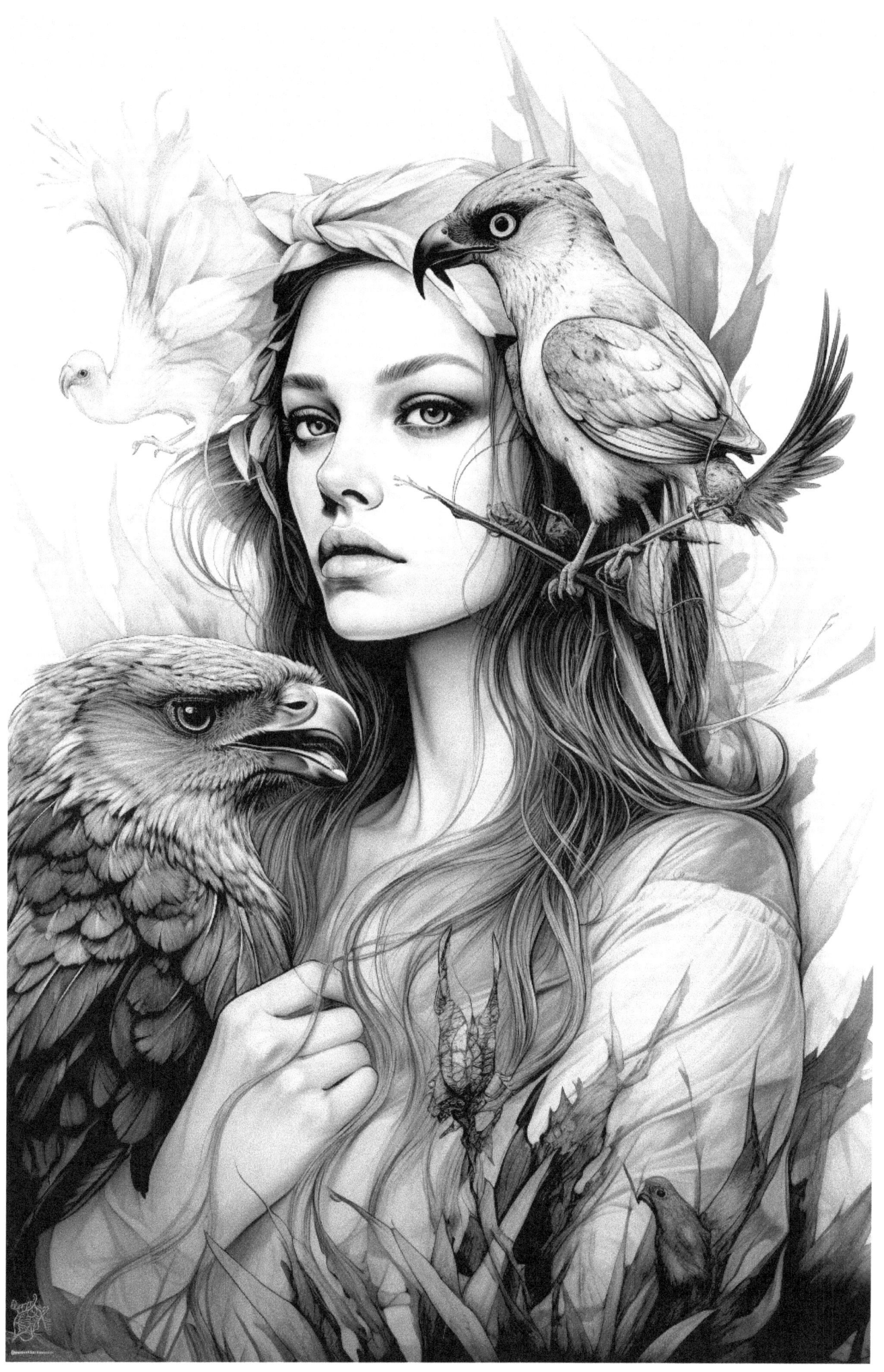

Forest Fairies left this blank for you

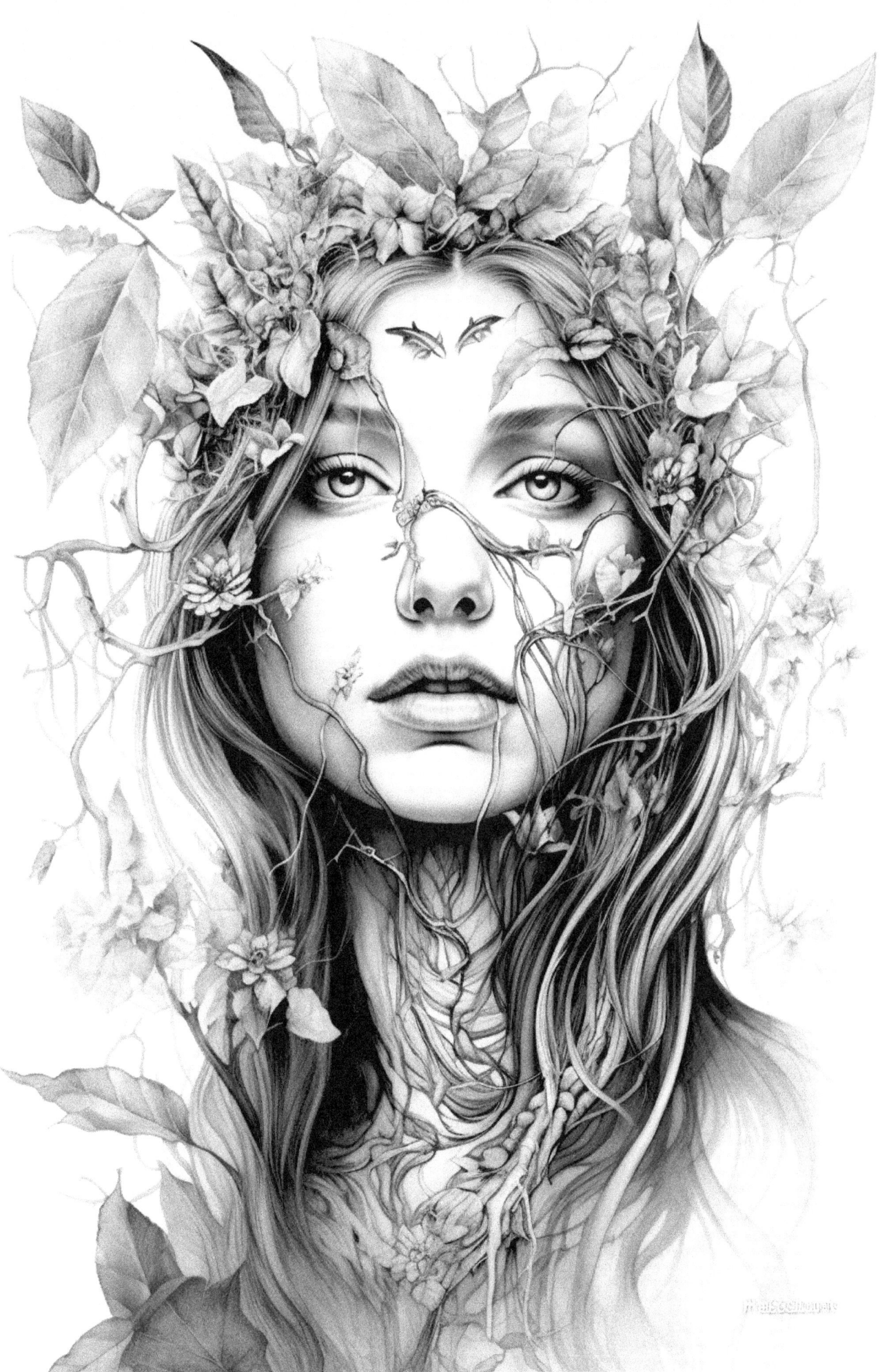

Forest Fairies left this blank for you

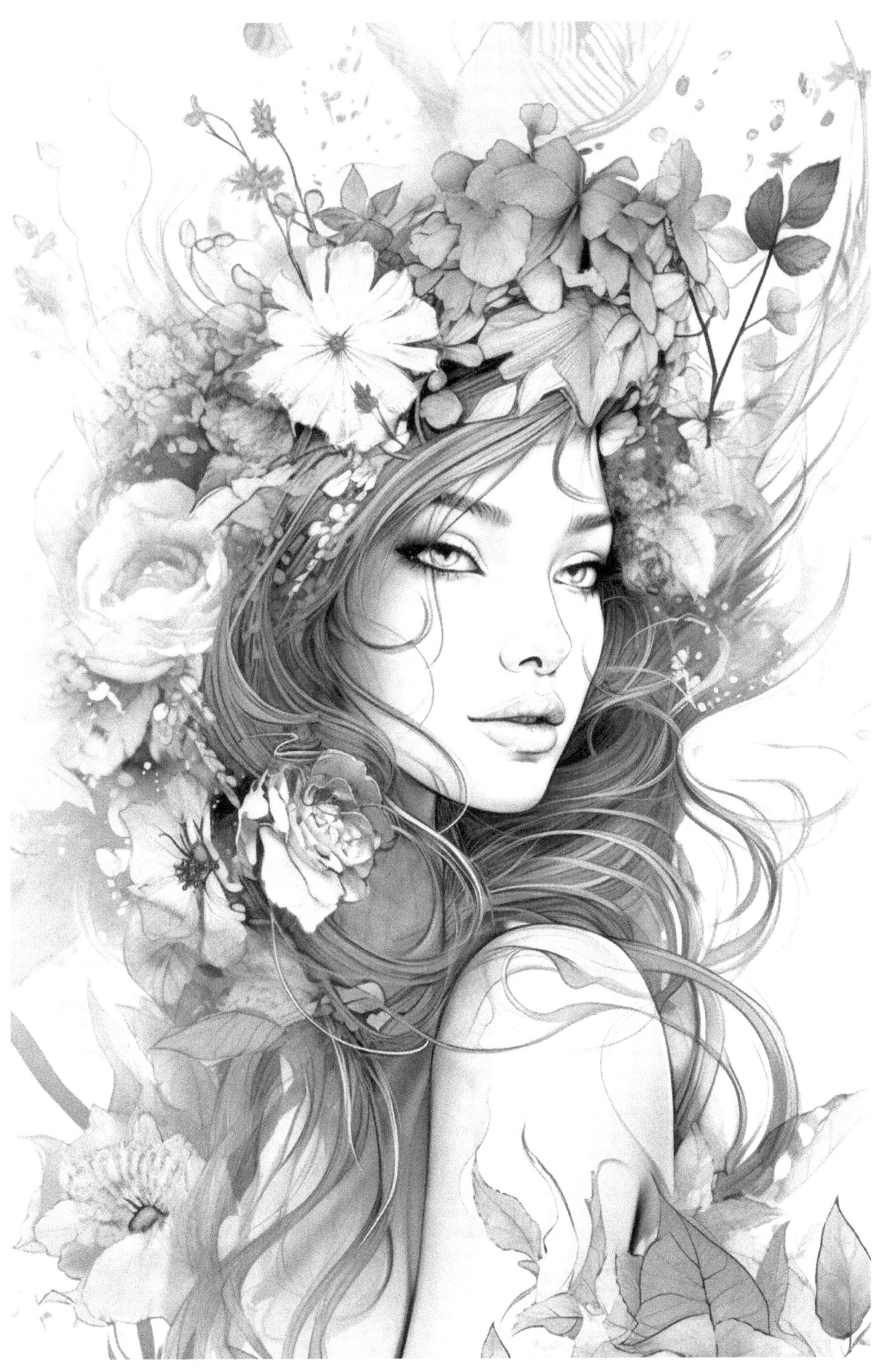

Forest Fairies left this blank for you

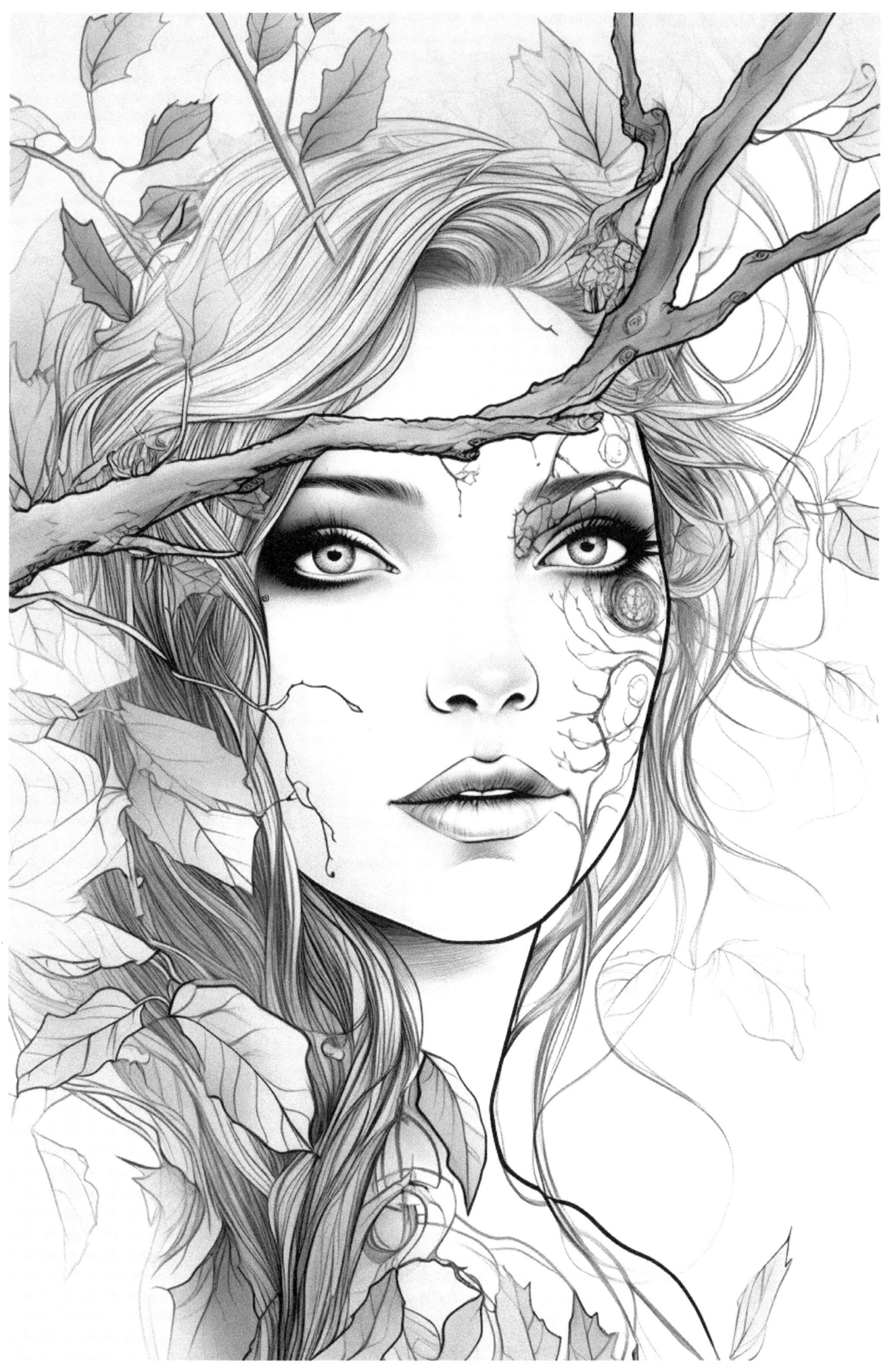

Forest Fairies left this blank for you

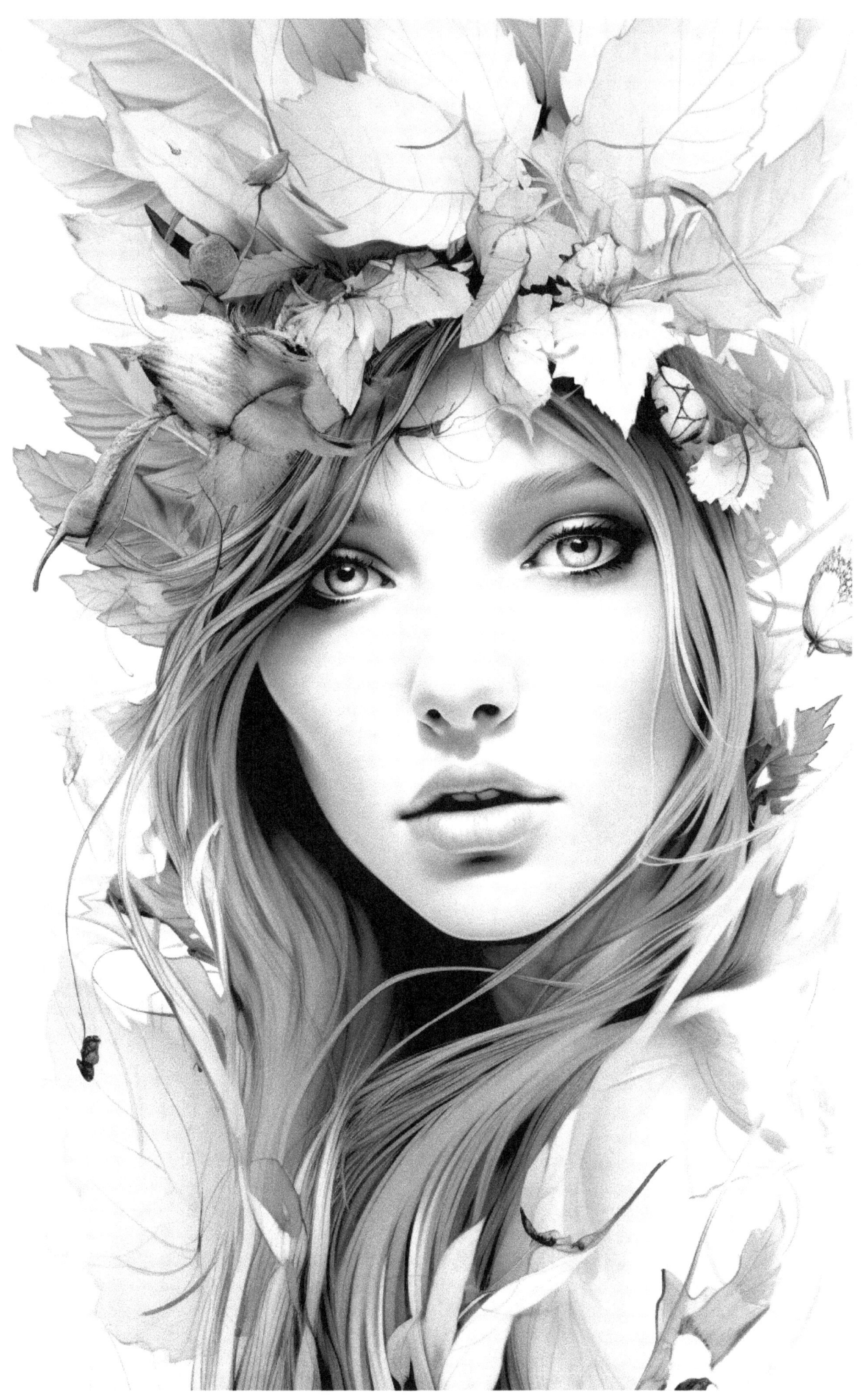

Forest Fairies left this blank for you

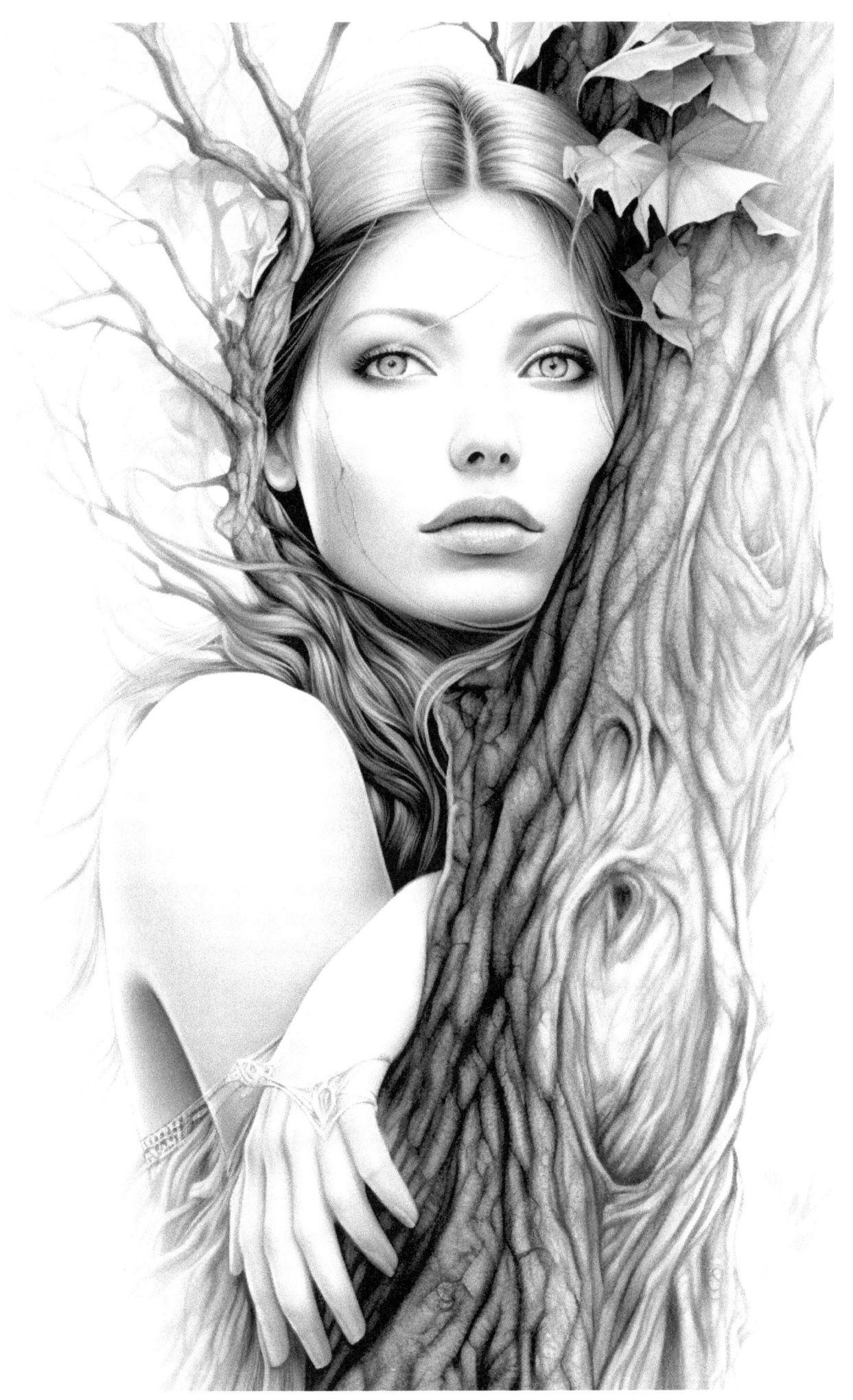

Forest Fairies left this blank for you

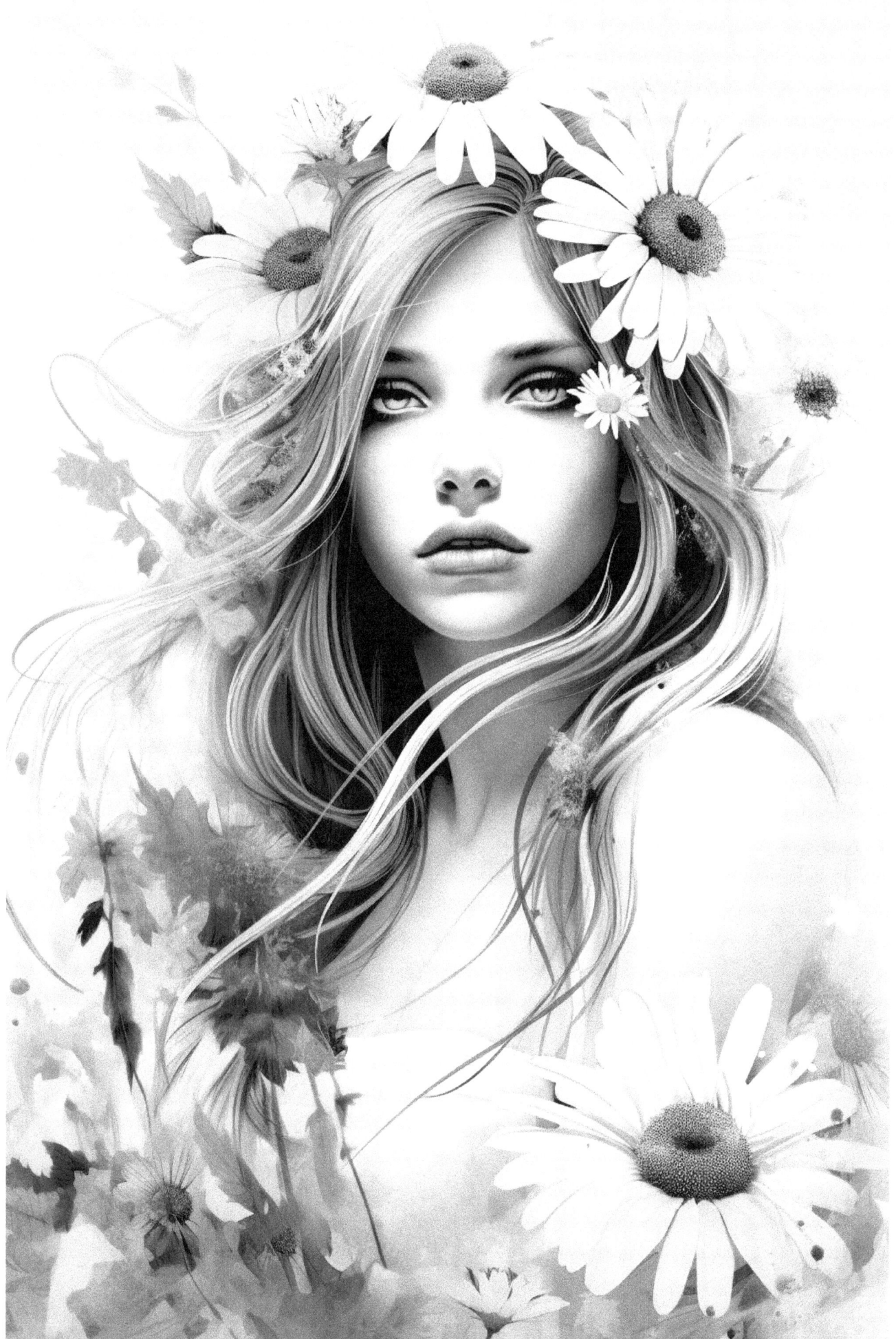

Forest Fairies left this blank for you

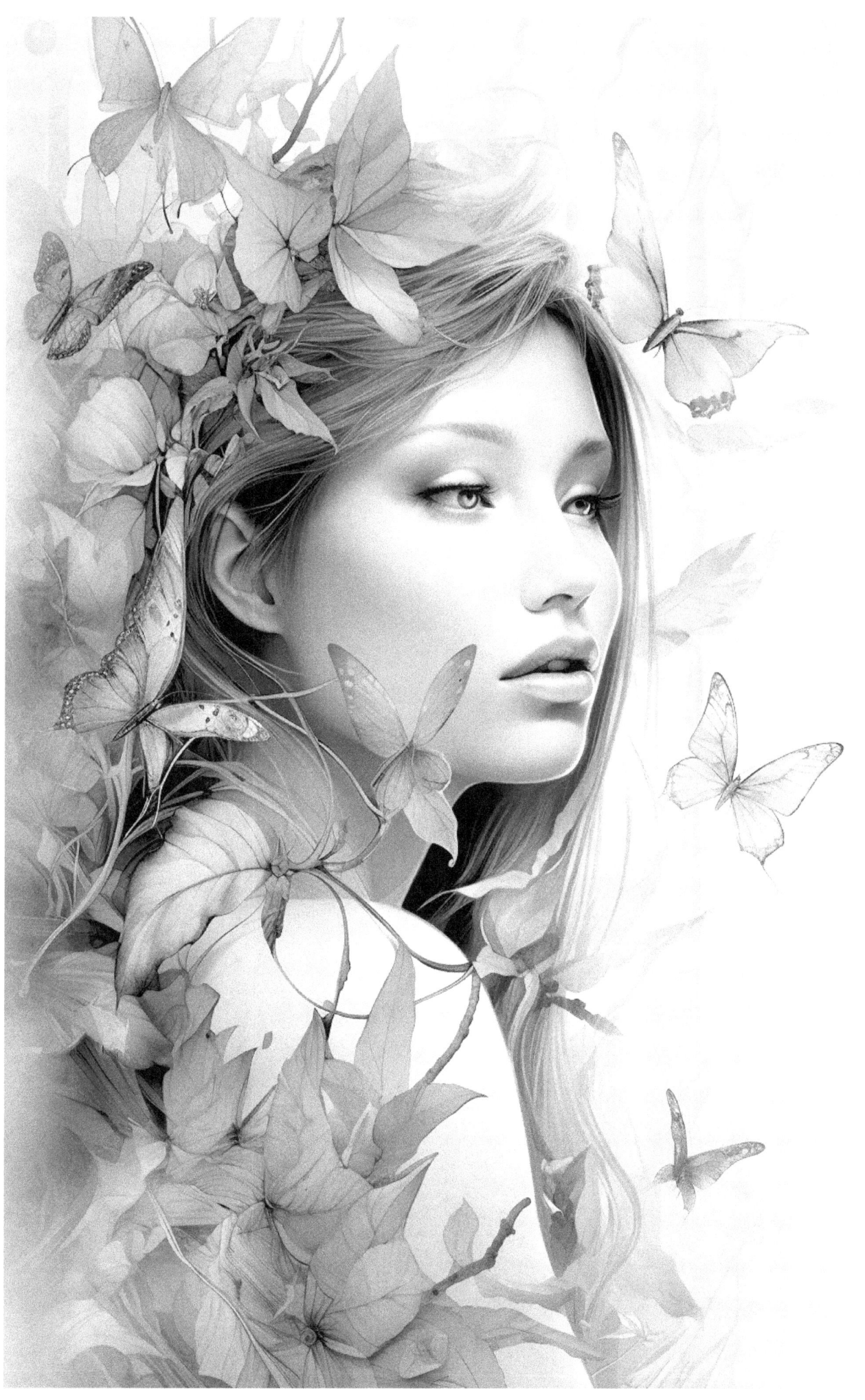

Forest Fairies left this blank for you

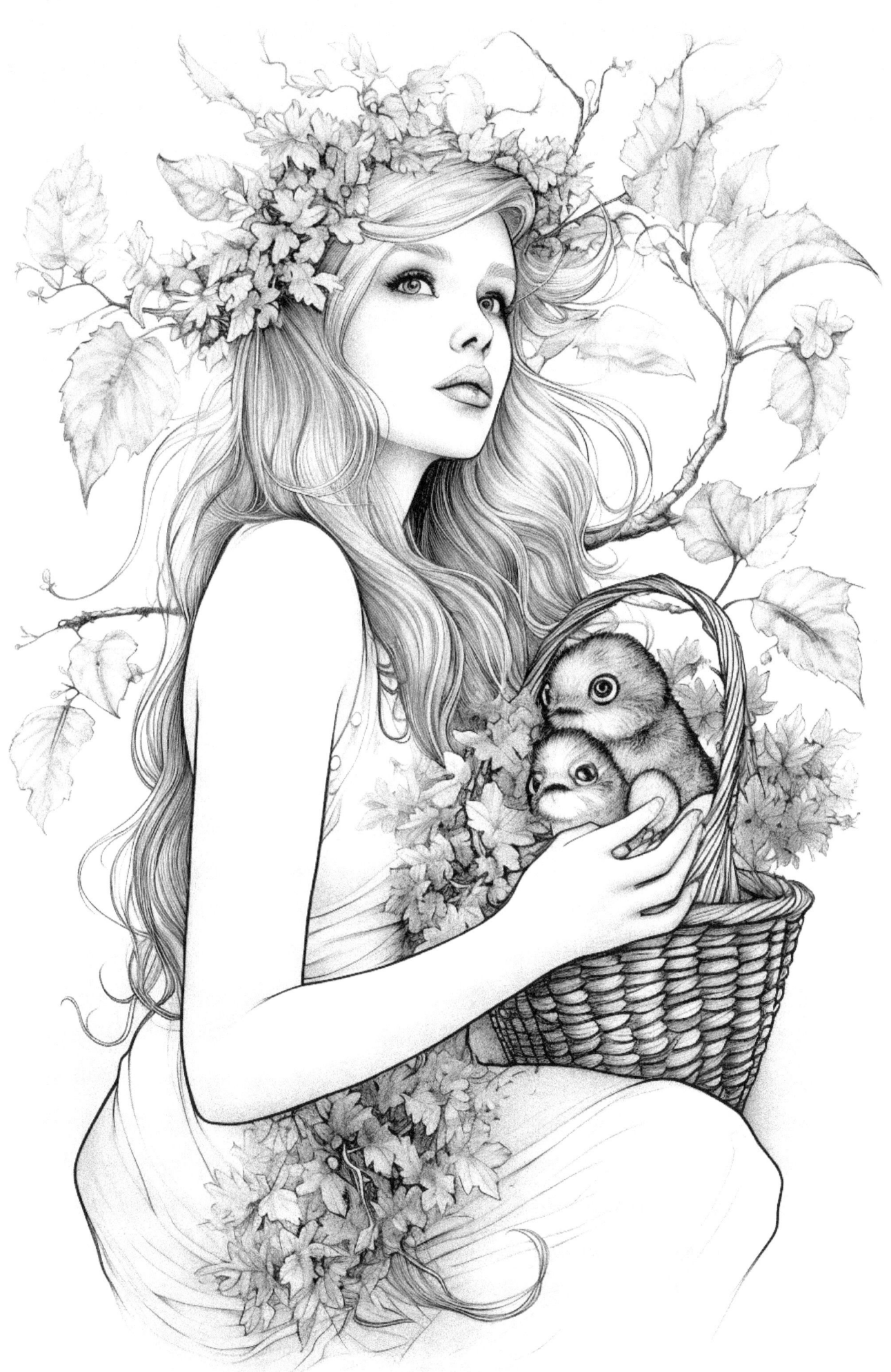

Forest Fairies left this blank for you

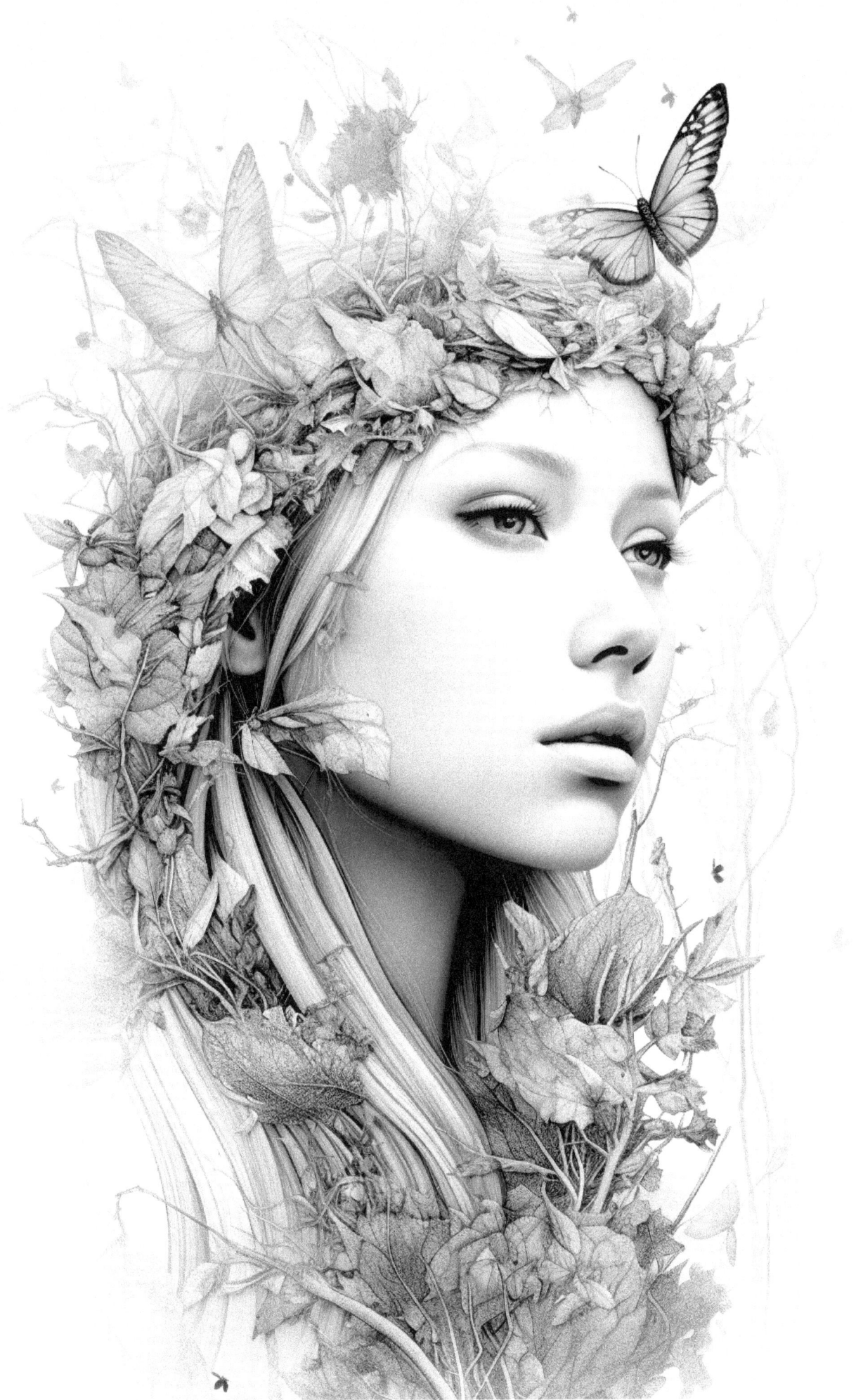

Forest Fairies left this blank for you

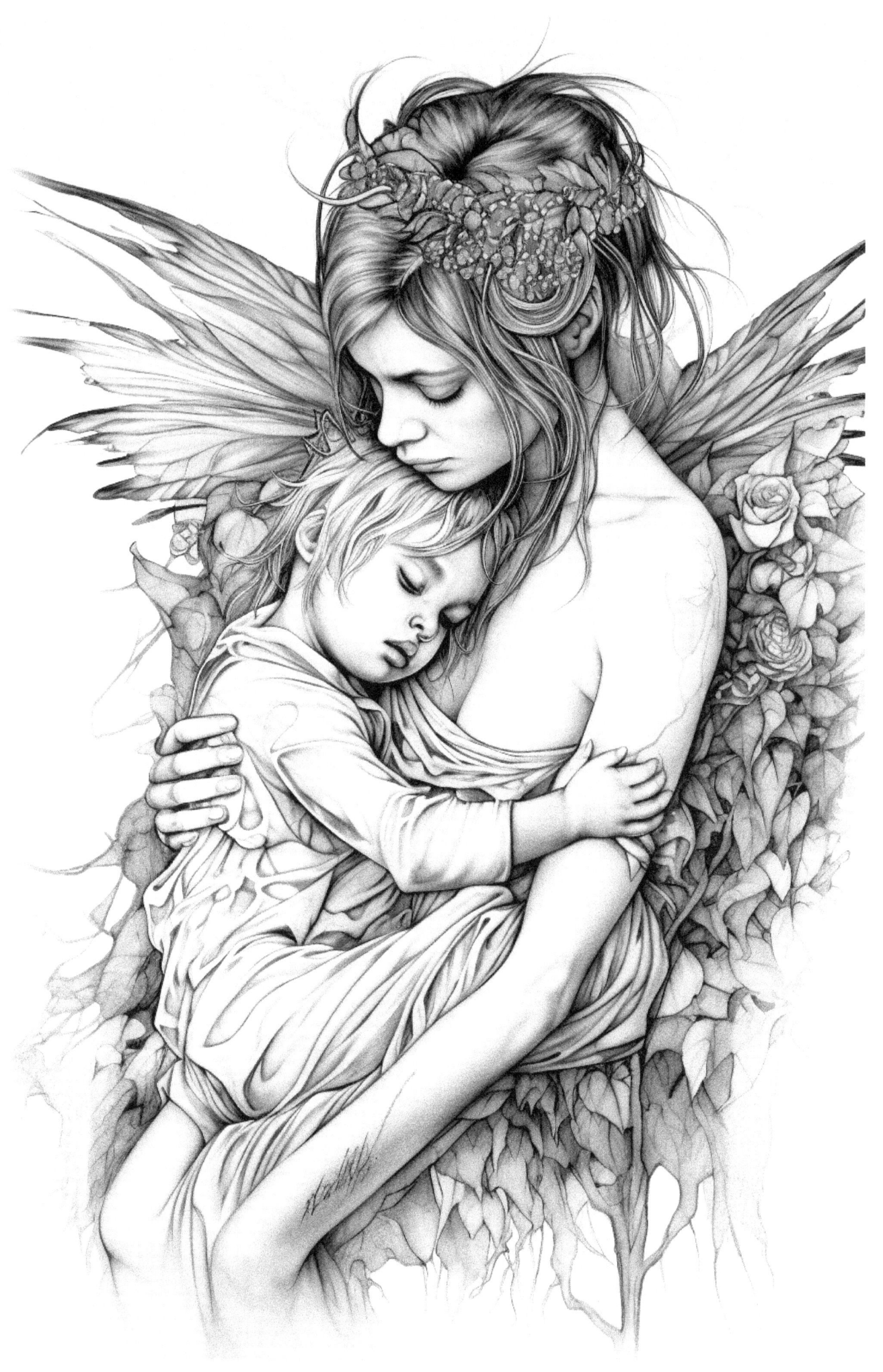

Forest Fairies left this blank for you

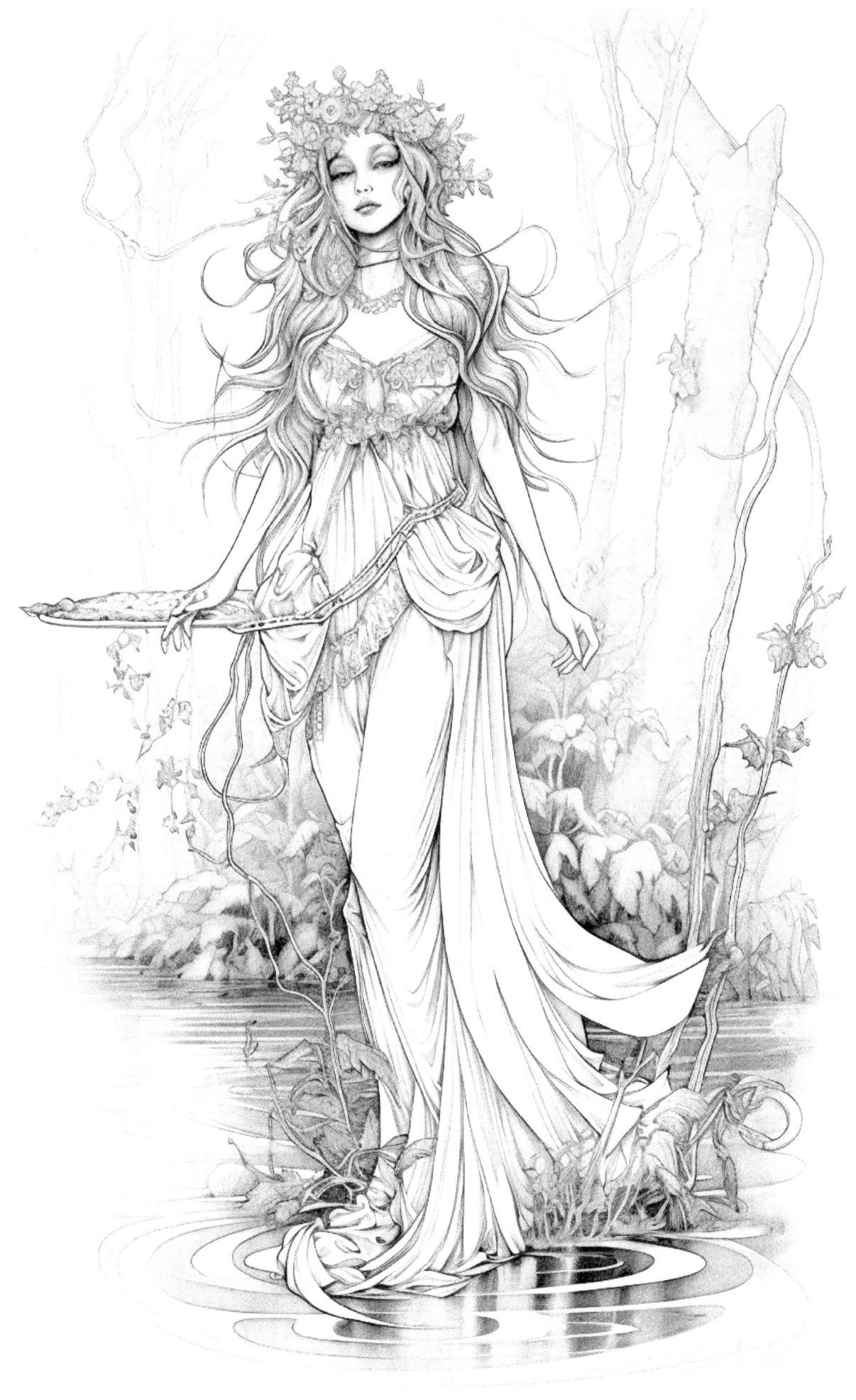

Forest Fairies left this blank for you

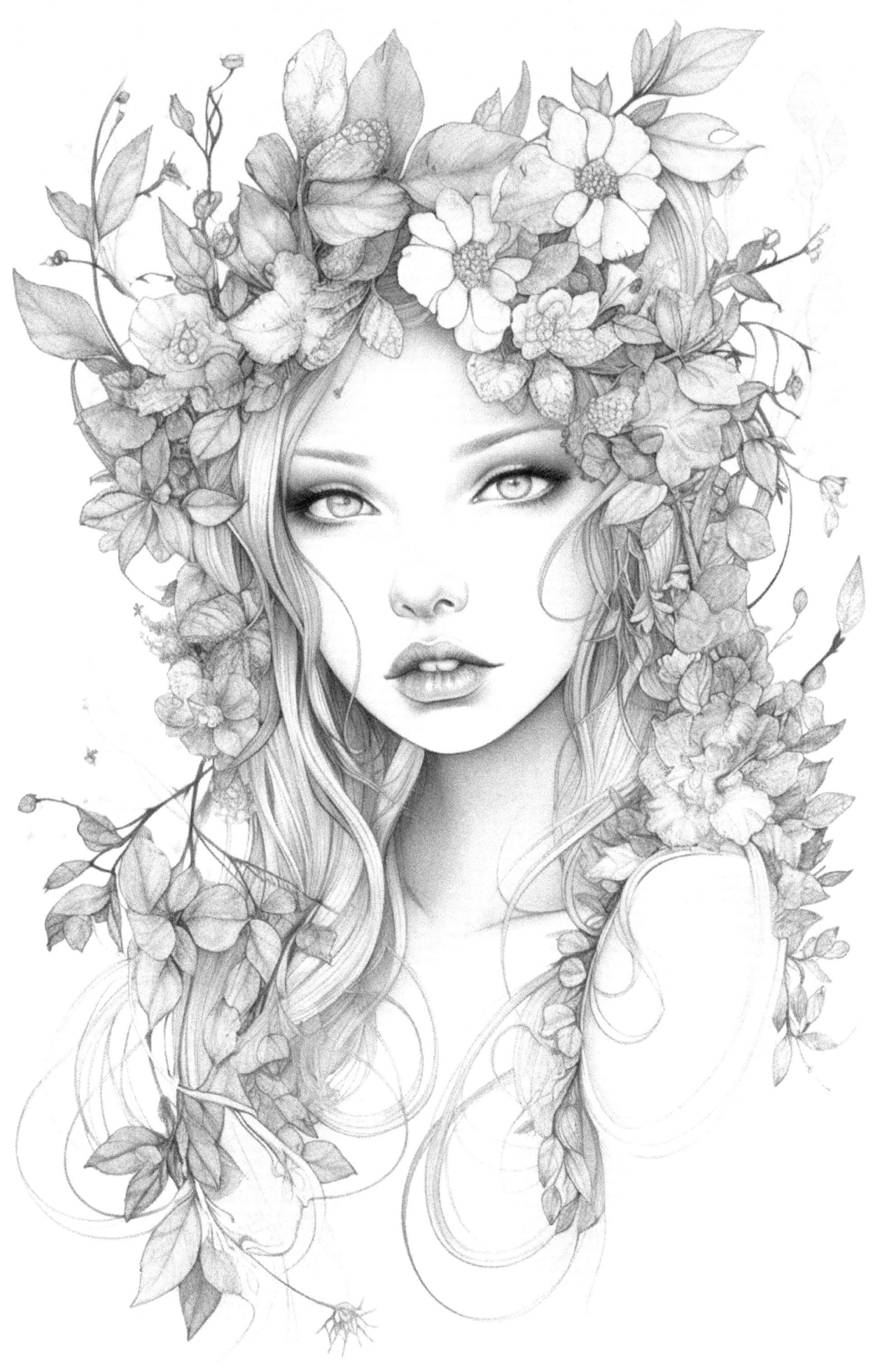

Forest Fairies left this blank for you

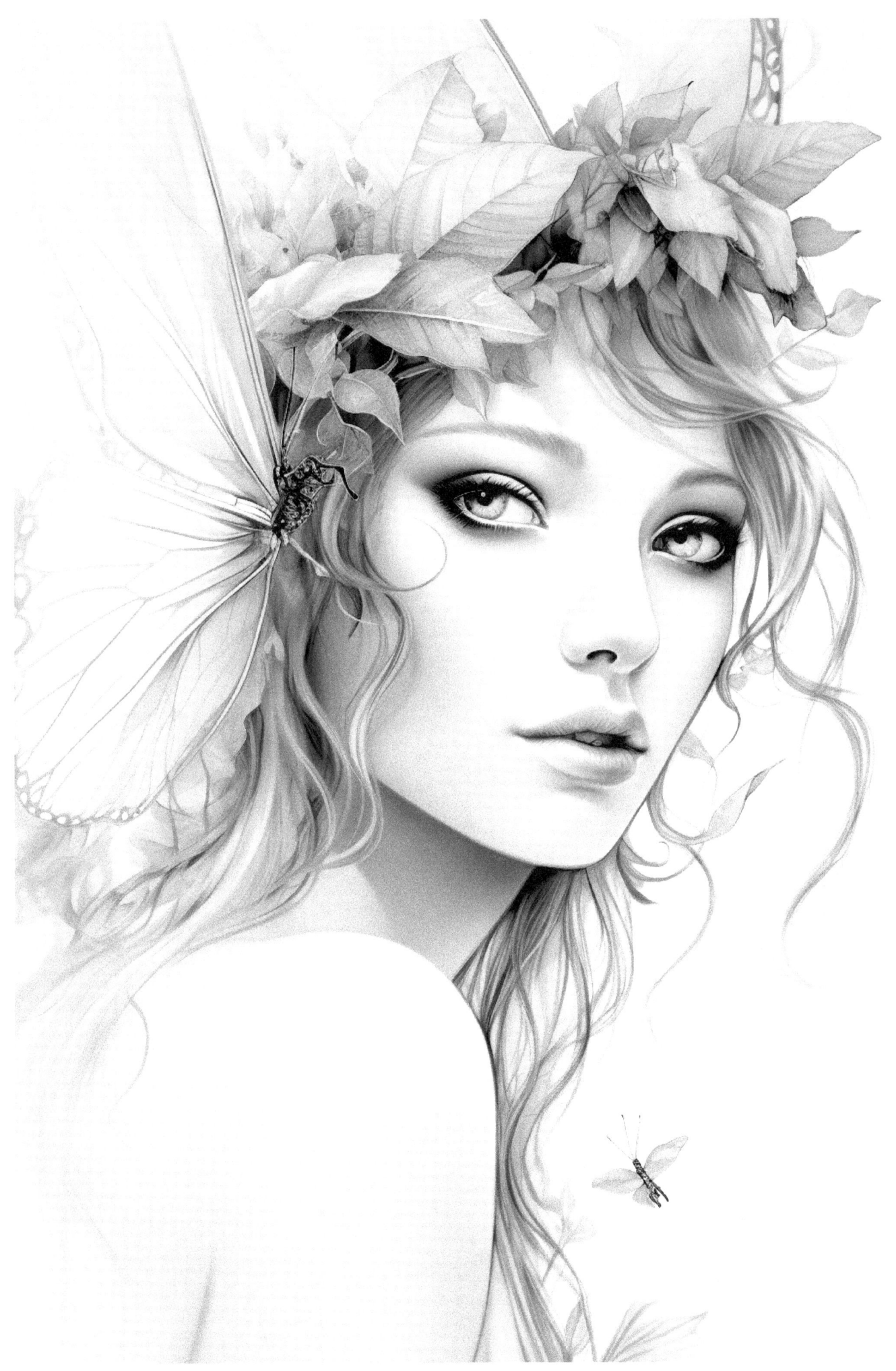

Forest Fairies left this blank for you

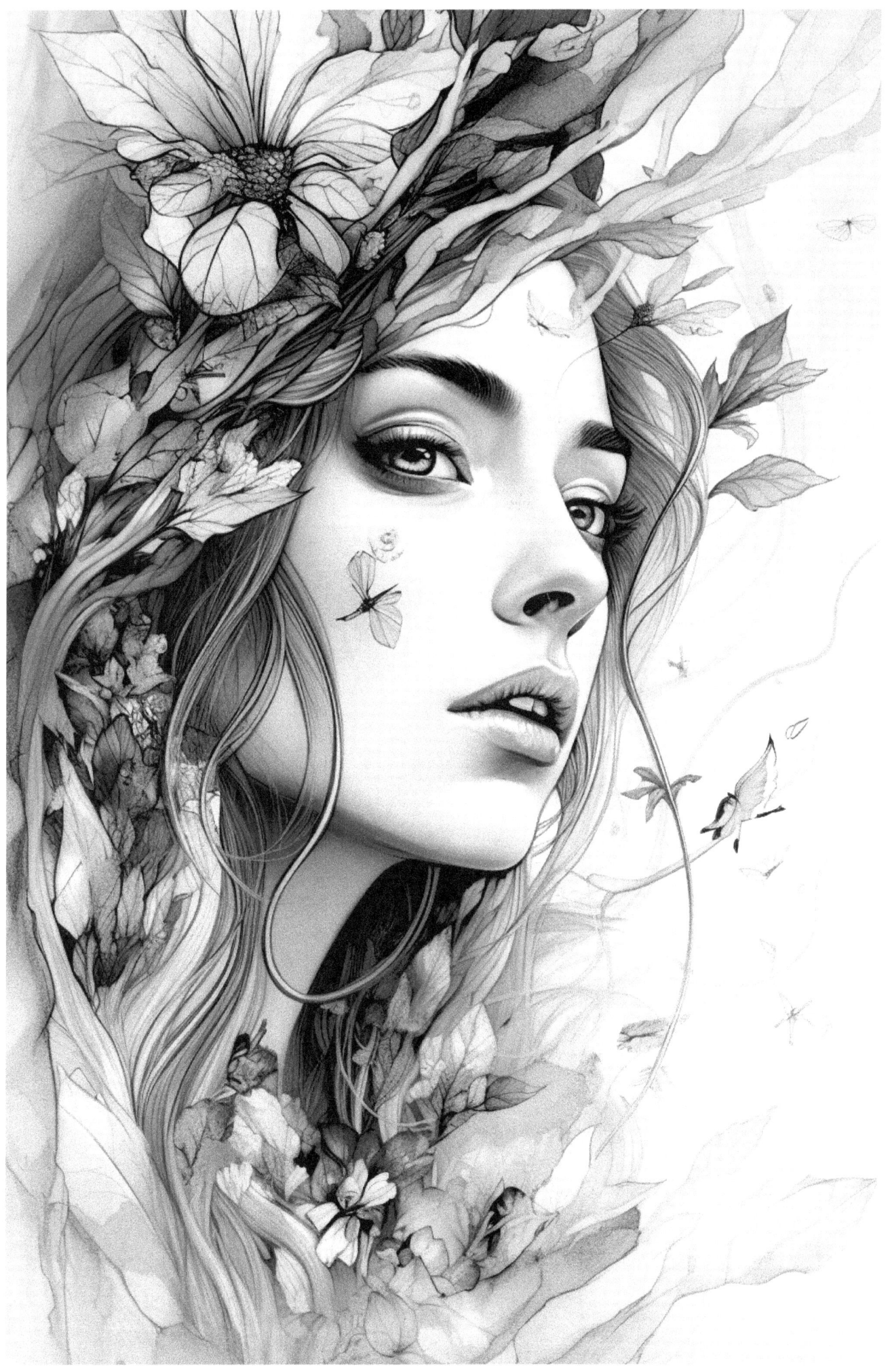

Forest Fairies left this blank for you

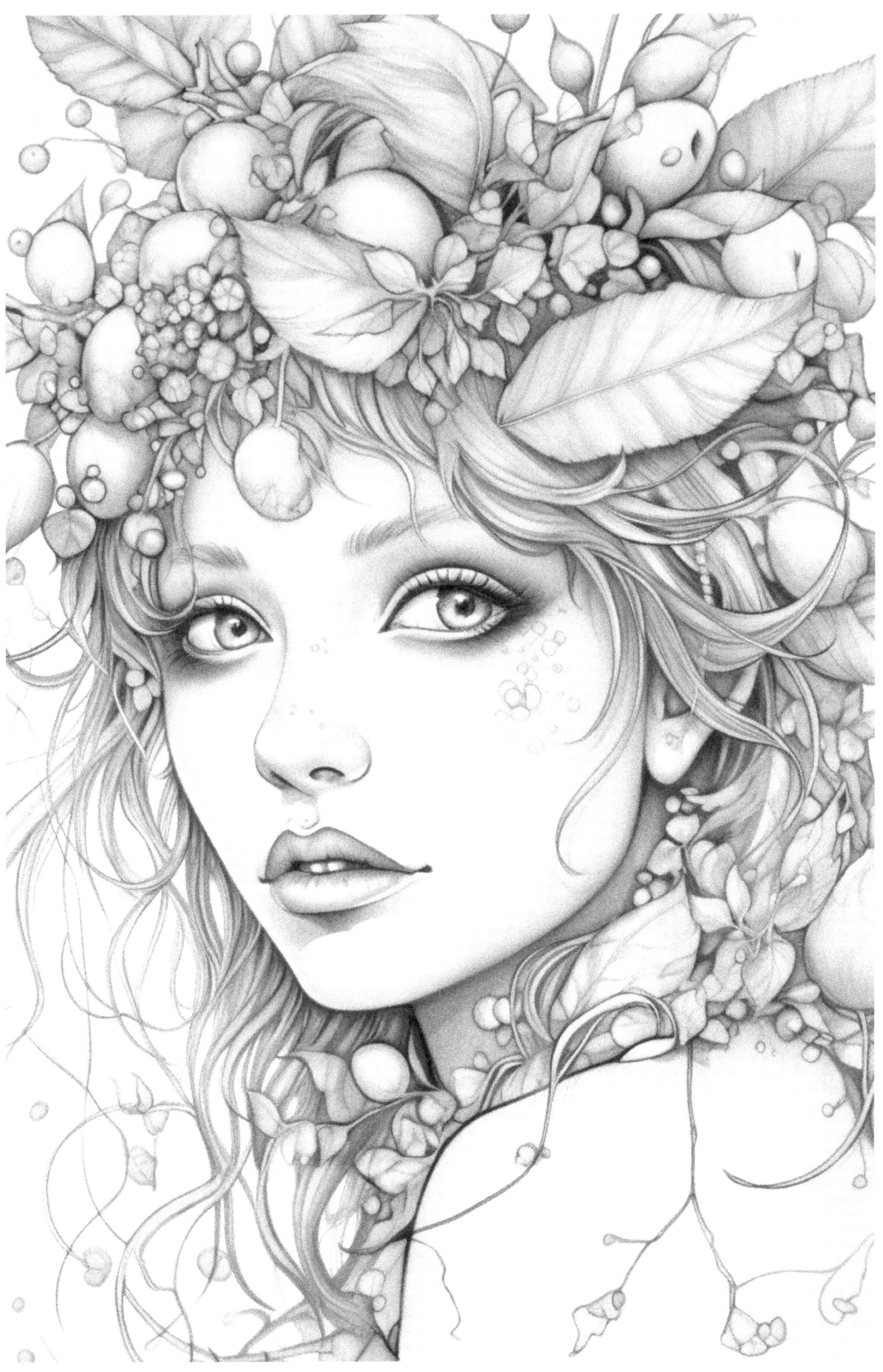

Forest Fairies left this blank for you

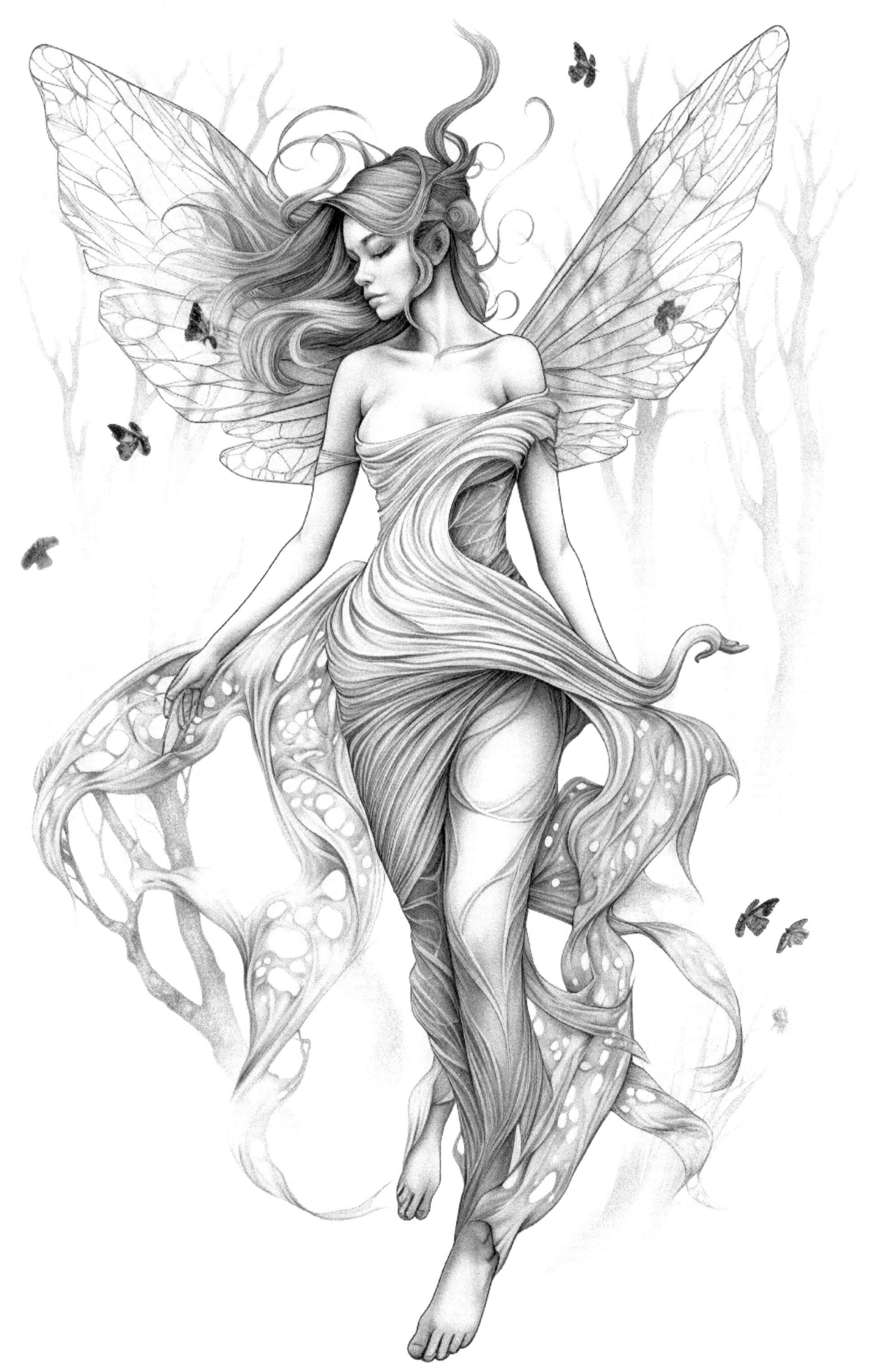

Forest Fairies left this blank for you

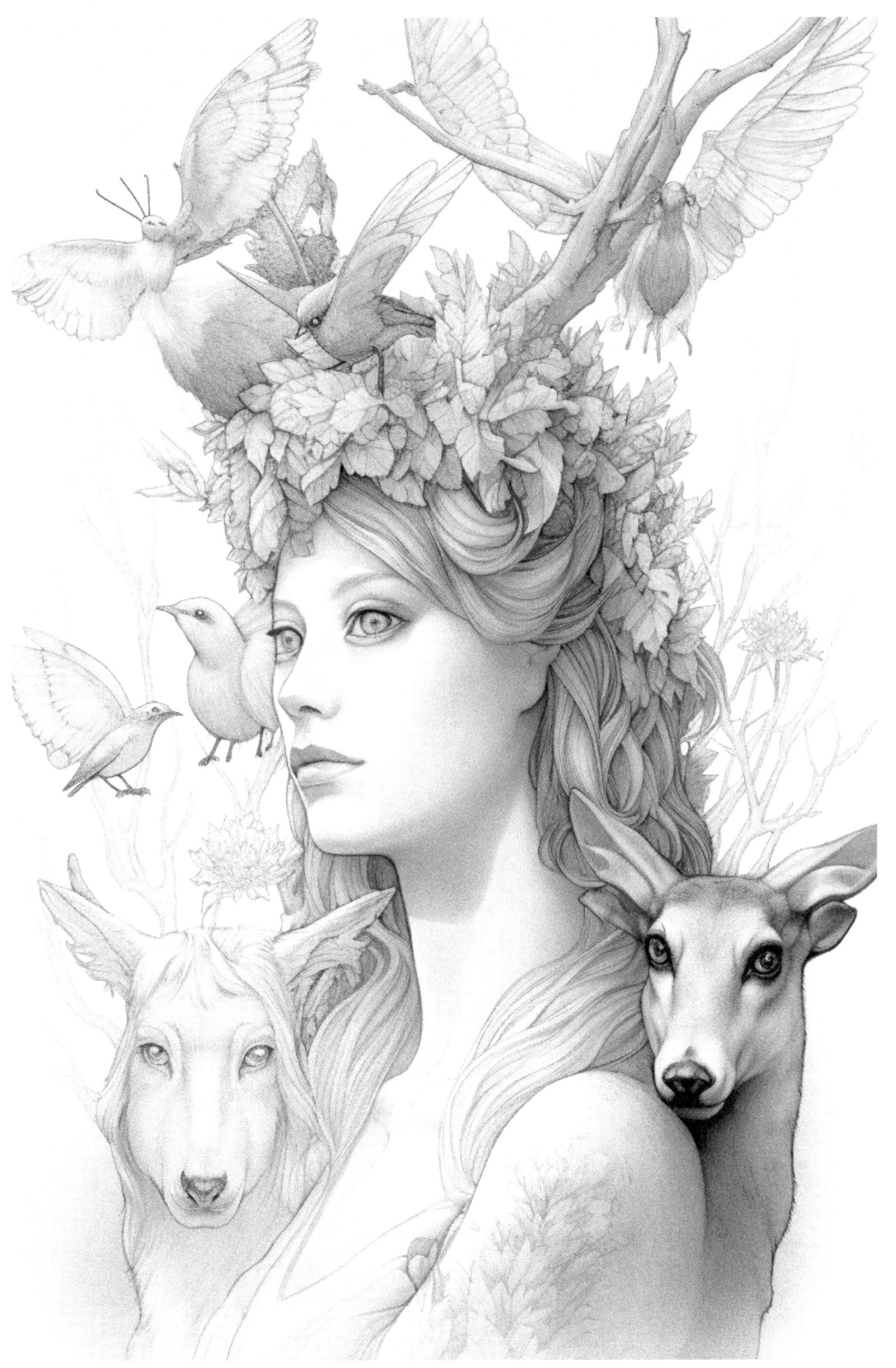

Forest Fairies left this blank for you

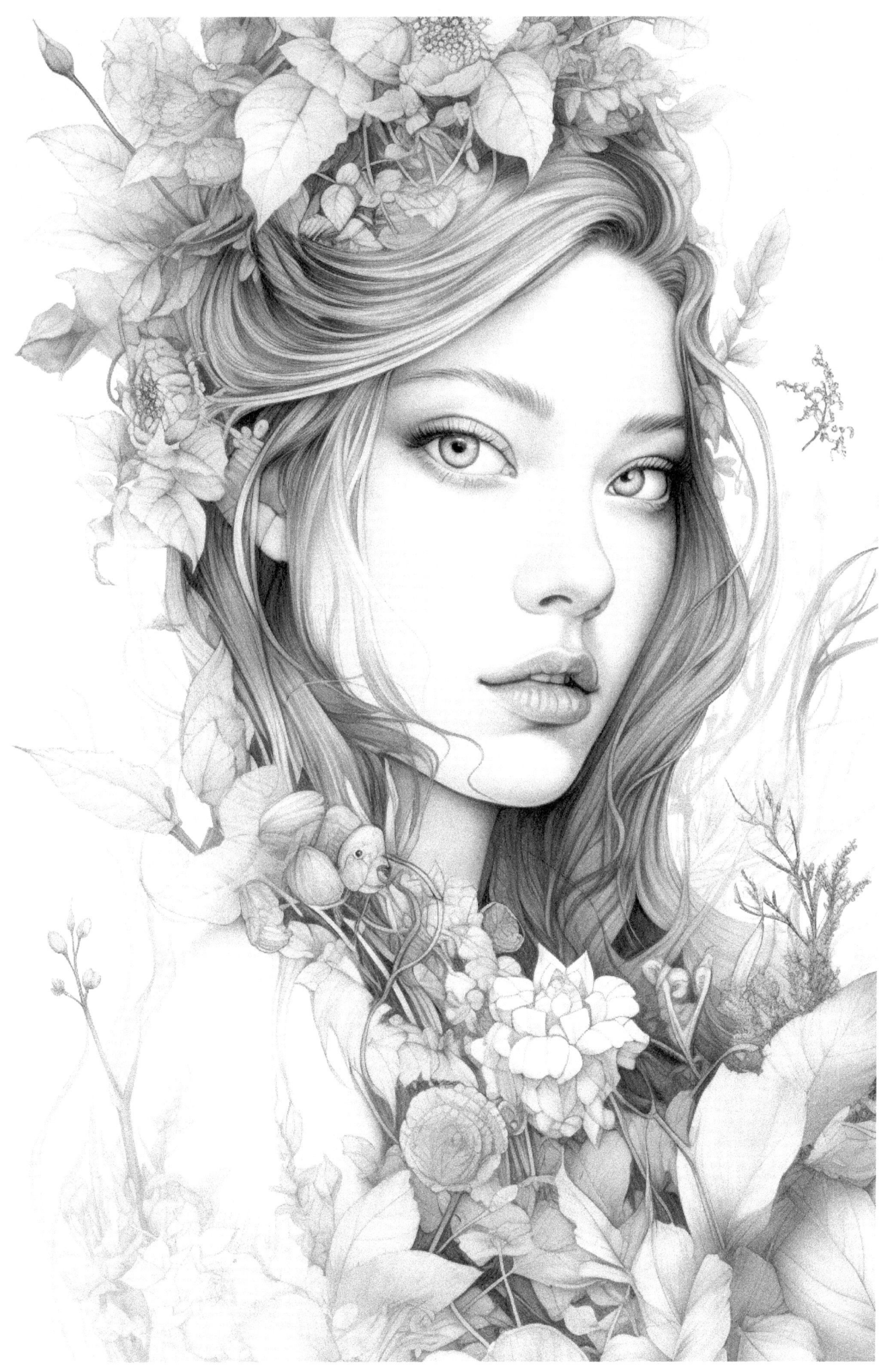

Forest Fairies left this blank for you

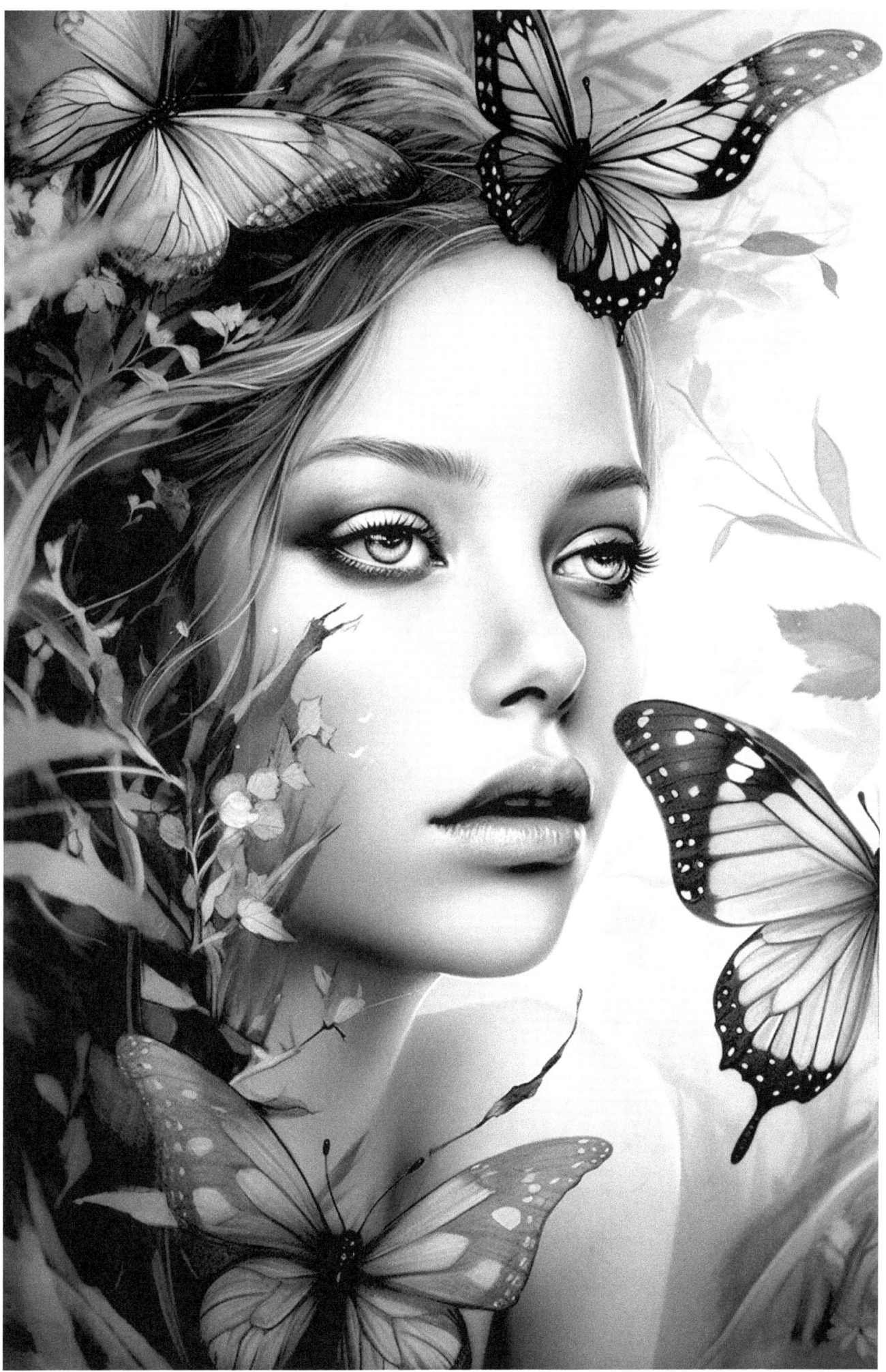

Forest Fairies left this blank for you

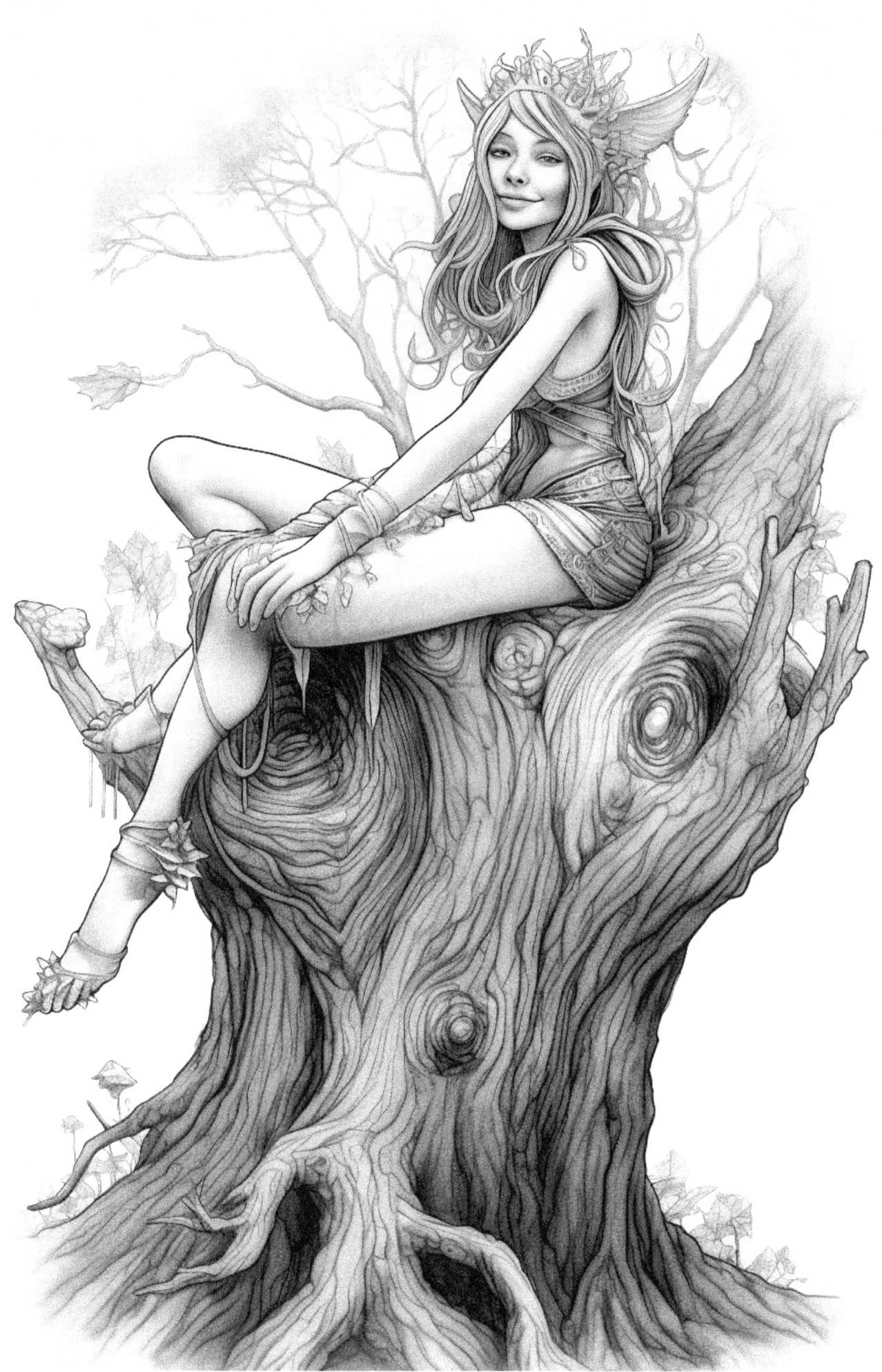

Forest Fairies left this blank for you

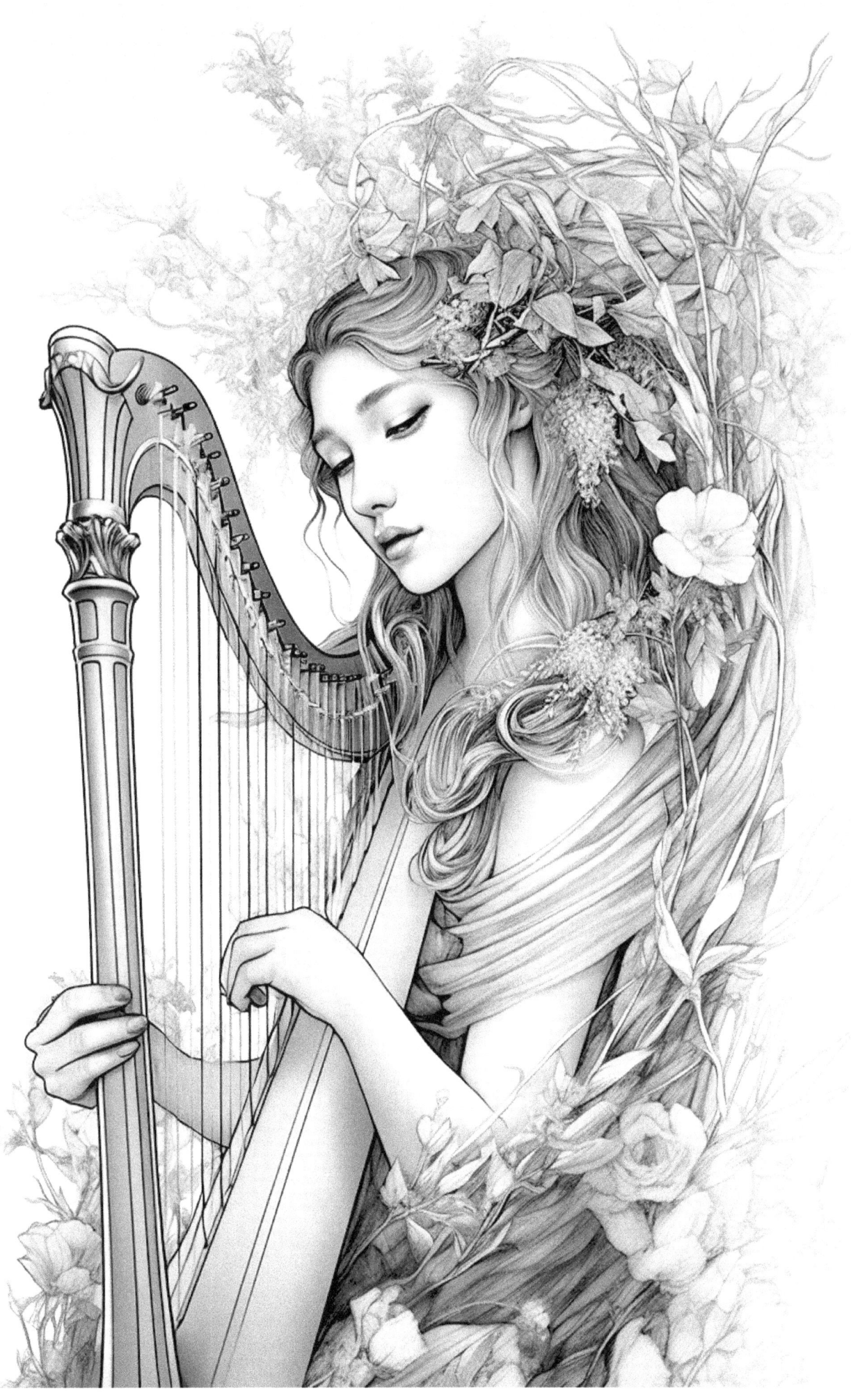

Forest Fairies left this blank for you

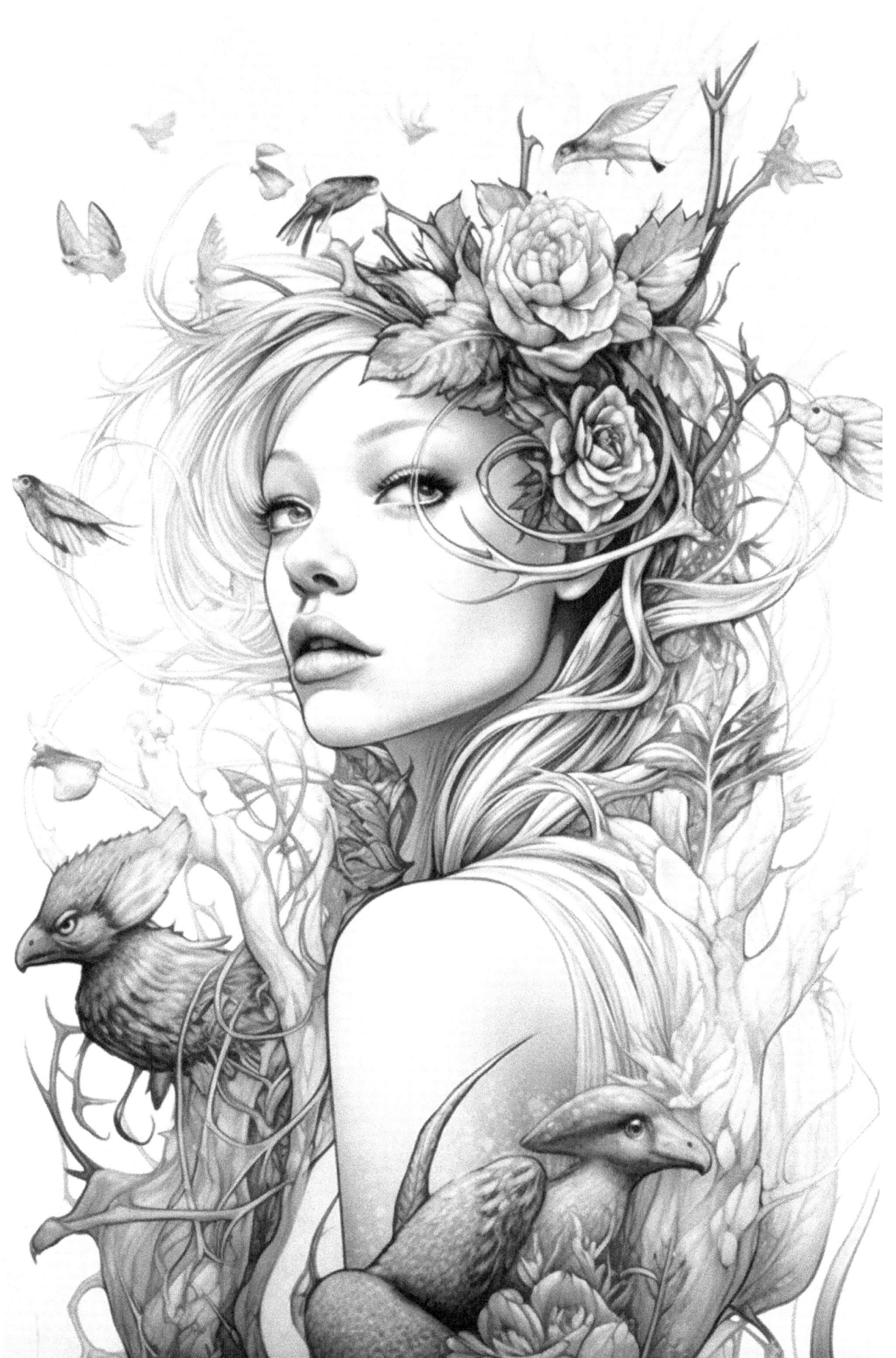

Forest Fairies left this blank for you

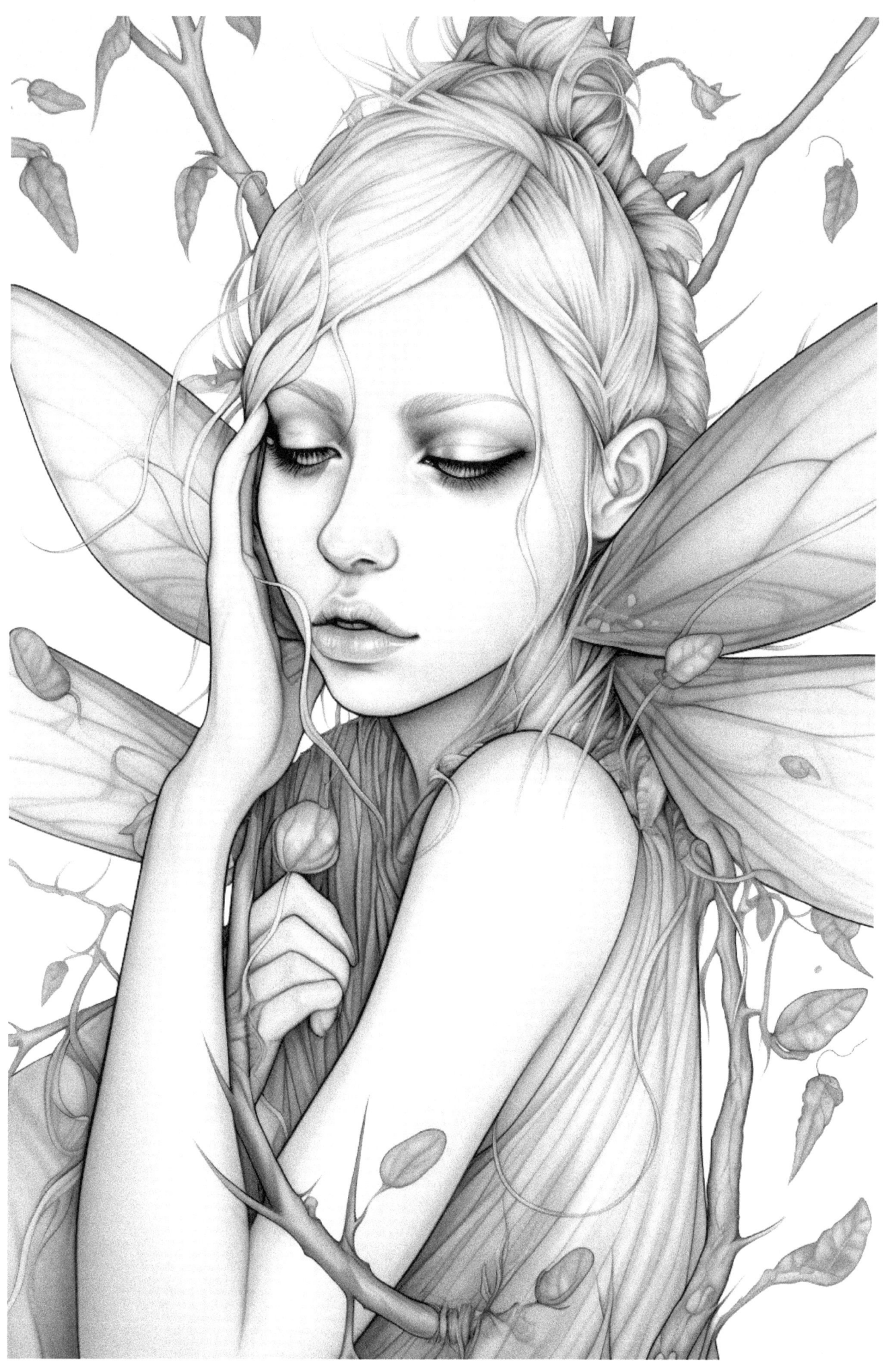

Forest Fairies left this blank for you

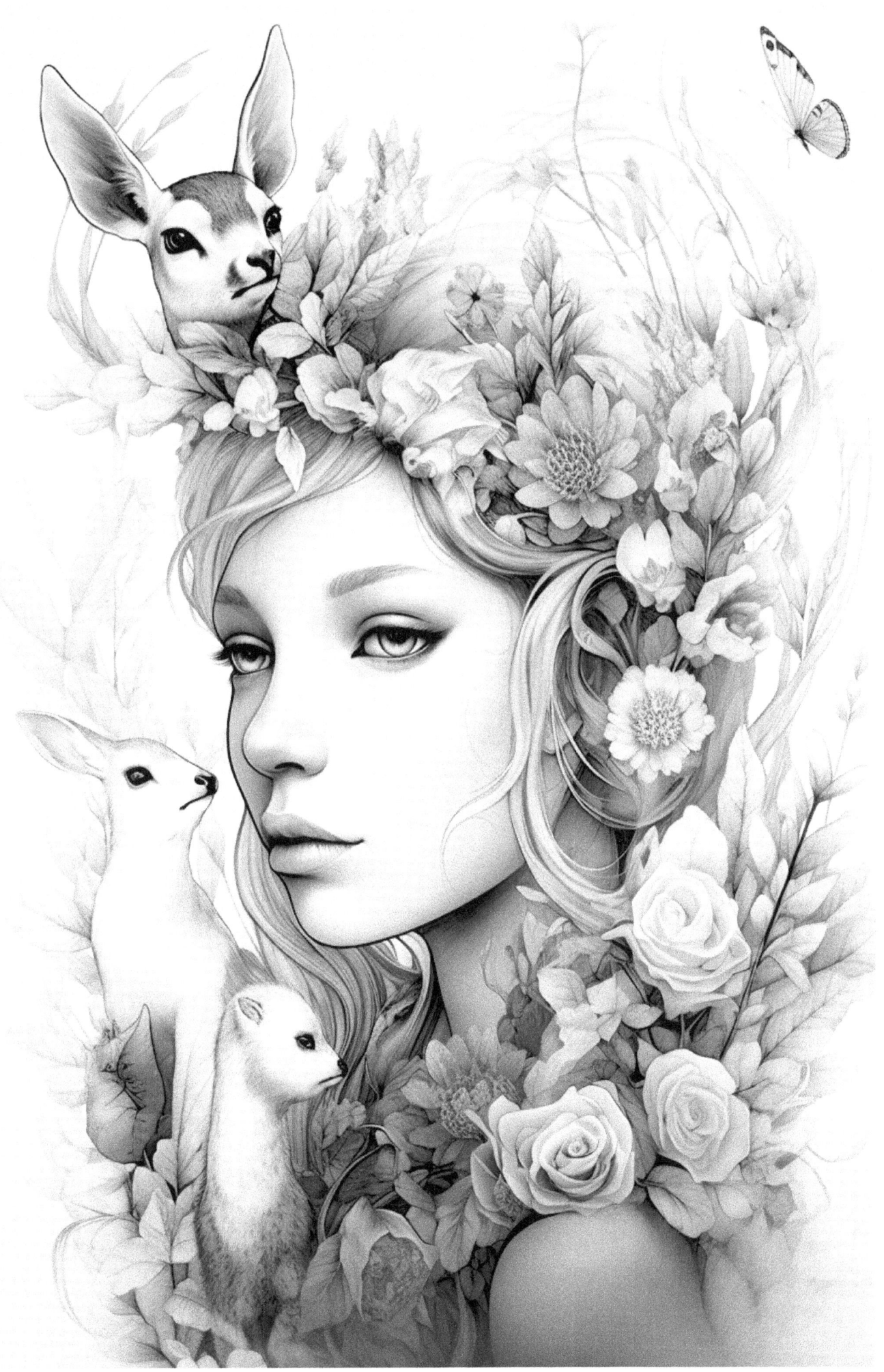

Forest Fairies left this blank for you

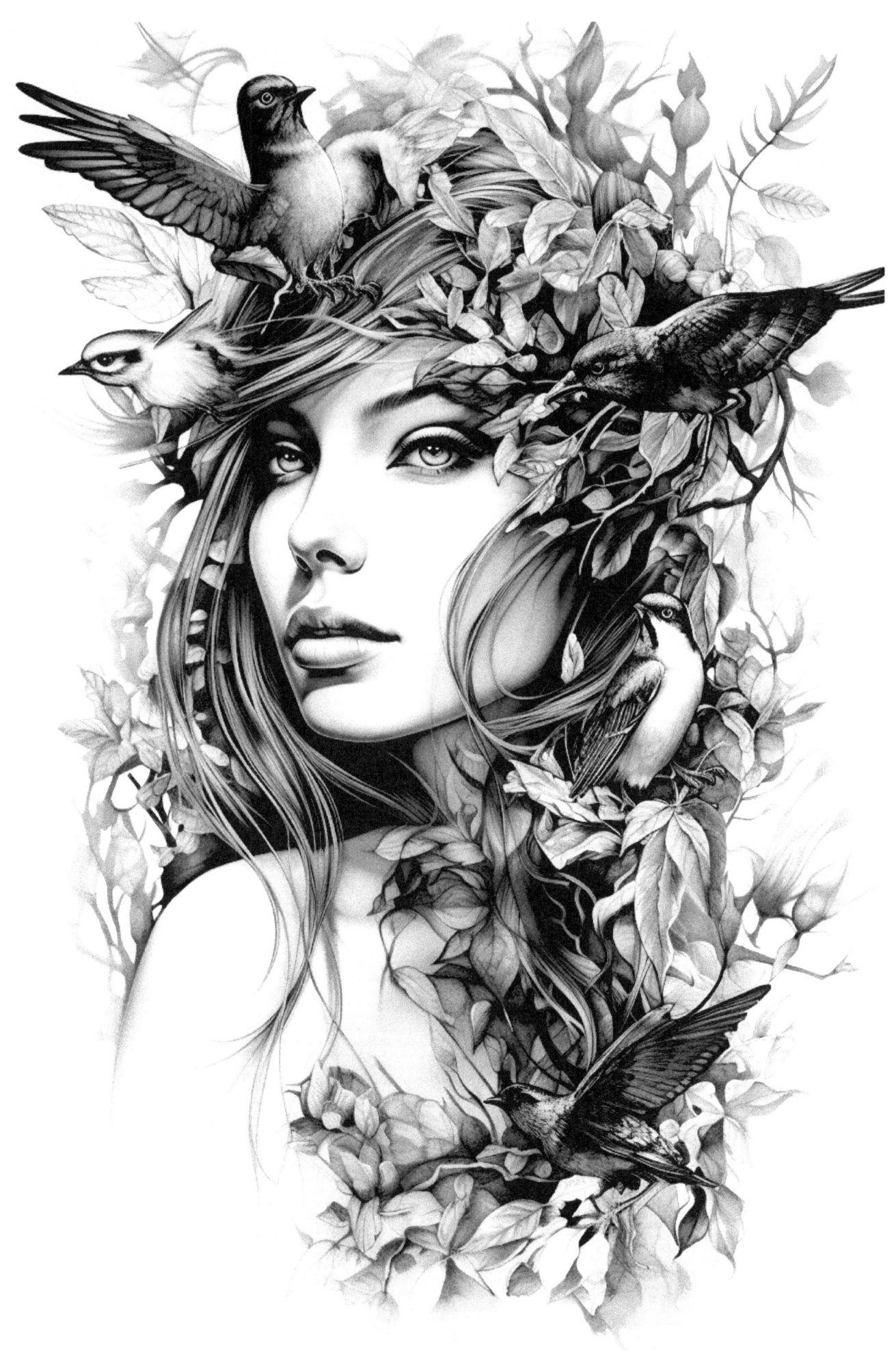

Forest Fairies left this blank for you

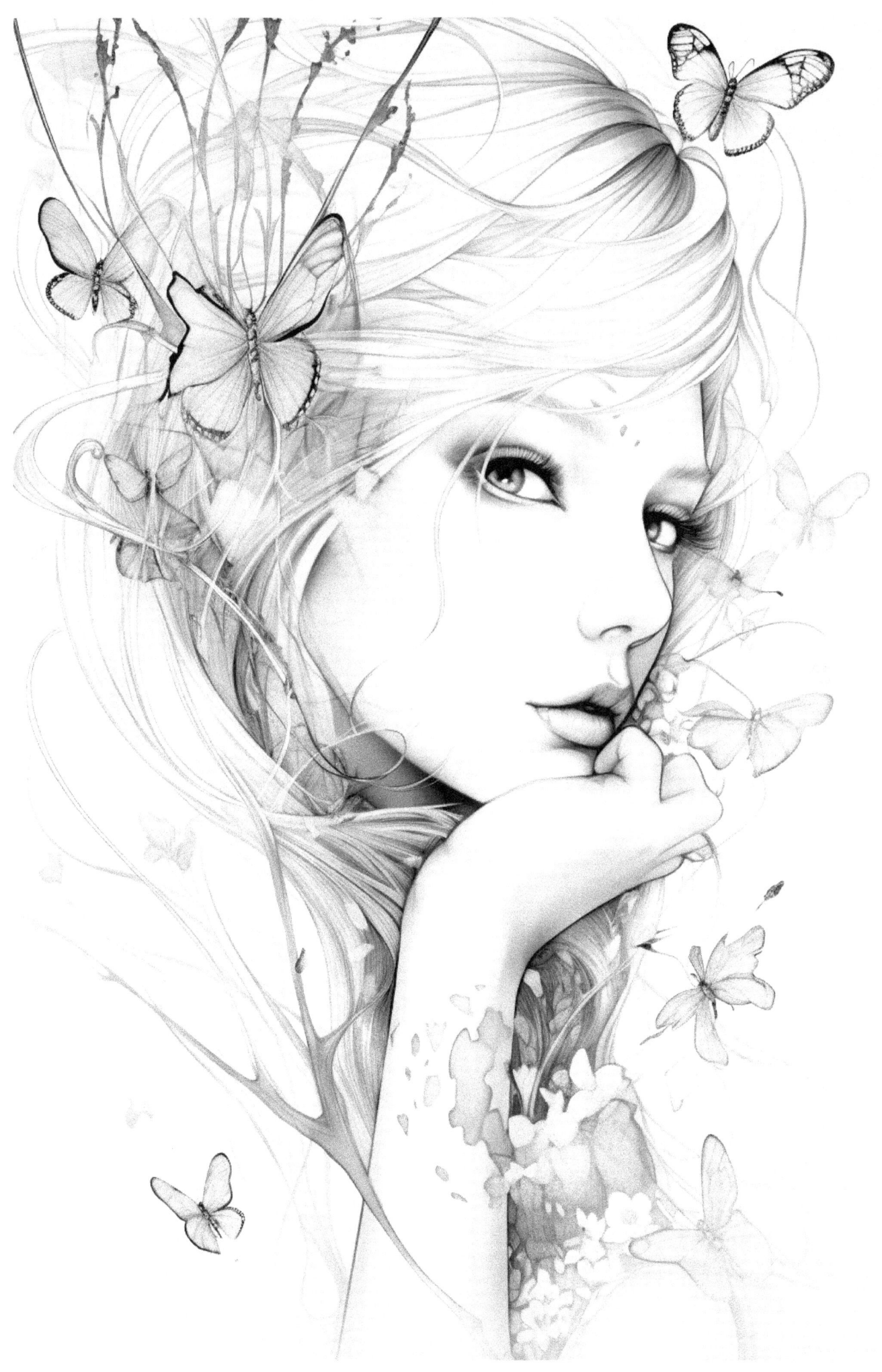

Forest Fairies left this blank for you

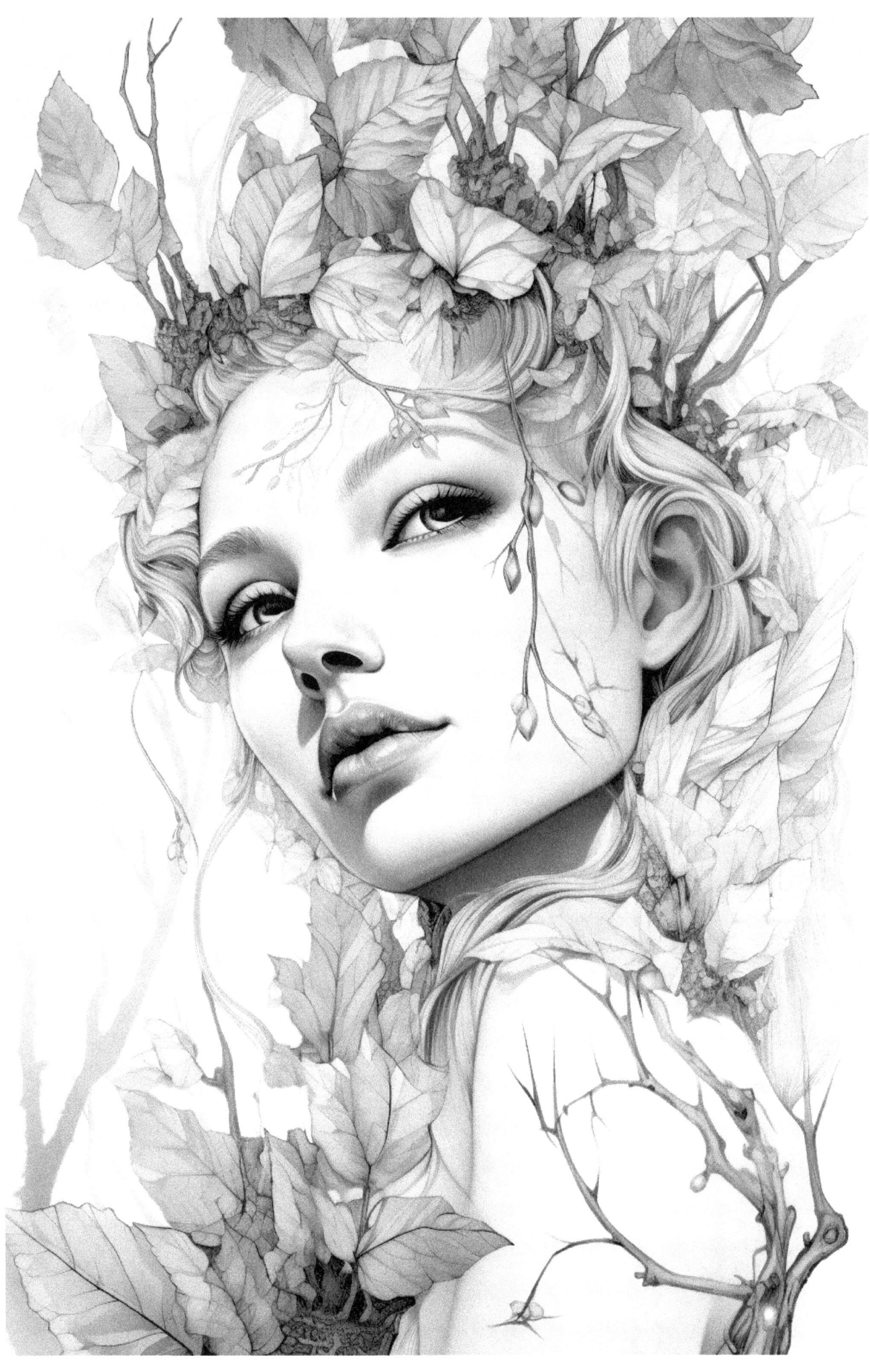

We hope you had as much fun coloring in the pages, as we had creating them!

If so, please let us and others know by leaving a review on Amazon :-)

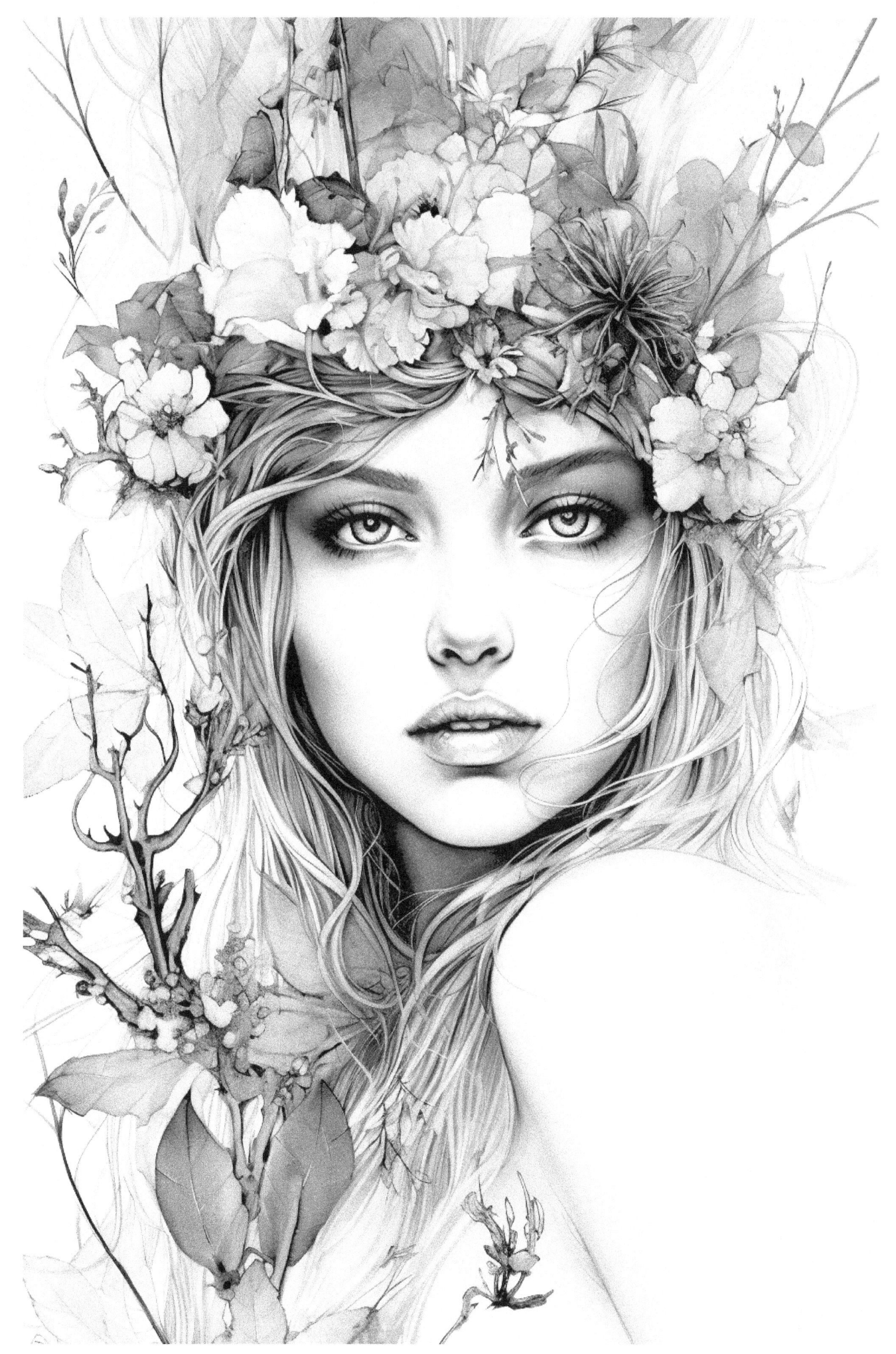

www.ingramcontent.com/pod-product-compliance
Lightning Source LLC
Chambersburg PA
CBHW080844220526
45467CB00008B/2390